Son of Man, Son of God

By

Maurice Kennedy

Copyright

Copyright 2021 Maurice Kennedy

Son of Man, Son of God

This is the author's original work. Scripture references taken from the following Bible translations (used with permission):

Scripture quotations marked NKJV New King James Version of the Bible. © 1982 by Thomas Nelson, Inc., publishers.

Scripture quotations marked KJV are from the King James Version of the Bible.

Scripture quotations marked CSB are from the Christian Standard Bible version.

Scripture quotations marked NLT are from the New Living Translation.

Scripture quotations marked NIV are from the New International Version.

Scripture quotations marked AMPC are from the Amplified Bible, Classic Edition

Scripture quotations marked ESV are form the English Standard Version

Scripture quotations marked AMP are from the Amplified Bible

Scripture quotations market BSB are from the Berean Study Bible

ISBN: 9798527830477

Book Cover and Editing by Dr Jacqueline Samuels

https://tinyurl.com/AuthorJNSamuels

To Anthony + Joy
with
Love
Maurice Kennedy

Table of Contents

Copyright ii
How to Use This Book and Guide v
Foreword vi
Acknowledgements ix
Introduction xi
Chapter 1: How Can This Be? 1
Chapter 2: My Genesis 6
Chapter 3: Who Am I? 11
Chapter 4: Why Son? 17
Chapter 5: Why Father? 22
Chapter 6: Jesus Son of Man? 27
Chapter 7: Jesus Son of God? 31
Chapter 8: A Sacred Moment 38
Chapter 9: Only Begotten Son 45
Chapter 10: Another Genesis 52
Chapter 11: Godhead Communications 58
Chapter 12: Son of God Versus Children of God - No opt out 65
Chapter 13: The Corporate Son of God 71
Chapter 14: He Does the Glory 79
Chapter 15: The Age of the Son 84
Chapter 16: A Matter of Identity 89
Chapter 17: The Spirit of antiChrist: A Hostile Environment 94
Chapter 18: Fully Resourced 101
Chapter 19: Perfect Army on Display 106
Chapter 20: Walking in Sonship 112
Chapter 21: Not in Conclusion 119
Course Facilitator's Guide 123
About the Author 127

How to Use This Book and Guide

This book is designed for you to work through as an individual and where possible, within a group. There are seven themed sessions, each covering 2-4 chapters. Some session topics may take longer to complete than others. That is perfectly fine. The aim of this guide is to help direct your focus within each study session.

Included at the end of each chapter are thought provoking questions and reflections to further inform your learning. Please use this to create your own reader's journal.

May the grace of God direct your study, and the Holy Spirit be your guide as you journey in Christ.

Foreword

It is impossible for God to do anything without knowing "the end from the beginning," When He said: "Let us make man in our image and likeness," He was looking beyond the first Adam to the culmination of this decree, namely, the Body of Christ. This was His "original intent." The processes of His dealings with mankind would inevitably yield this result when the age concluded.

Everything in both realms of creation (heaven and earth) was designed to enable and to support this outcome. When the purposes of creation were fully realized, there would be on the earth, a spiritual man comprised of many members who had attained to the "fullness of the stature that belongs to Christ." Such a person is described as a "mature man" who has grown up into the "fullness of Christ." There is no other definition of "the church" at the end of the age. The Father is to be put on display in the darkened times at the conclusion of the age in this glorious presentation of Himself. *"The Son is the radiance of His Father's glory and the exact representation of His father's being."*

Unfortunately, historic Christianity has looked to the escape of the church from the earth as a defeated army forced to withdraw from the field of combat. It has placed its hope in being successfully evacuated. In the absence of a theology of the church growing up and becoming mature, there is no alternative to being rescued "in the nick of time." This idea leaves the original intent unfulfilled until we go to heaven. The true horror of this perspective is not only that it ignores the divine mandate, it also leaves the people of God in a dreadful state of unpreparedness and abandons altogether the heavenly mandate.

The spiritual body was always meant to grow up in a manner similar to that of the natural body. Both are initially born. "That which is born of flesh is flesh, and that which is born of spirit is spirit." One who is born of natural parentage is received into a natural family. The role of a natural father is to lead and direct the growth of that child to adulthood and a sufficient maturity to function as an adult, as well as carry on family purposes trans-generationally. Unfortunately, the corruption of human culture has replaced this model with the culture of orphans with no reference to a father modelled after God the Father. Such a concept is only vaguely referenced in old 'church hymns'. Nevertheless, the original intent was meant to be structured around spiritual Sonship to God as Father, and a spiritual family headed by a mature father who would teach and train the sons under his care to become mature.

It is impossible to relate this concept to the present-day church. It neither sees the central principle of sonship nor pretends that maturity of the believers in the pews is even a possibility to be considered. The evidence shows that the members are in perpetual stages of infancy while the church itself lurches from one extreme social position to another like a drunken man unable to find his way home. The fact that it has become almost completely irrelevant is painfully apparent to all but the church itself. In its present state, the only option the church can entertain is to be rescued from the cascading events of the present age.

In the midst of this catastrophe, God has been quietly raising up a people in whom He intends to fulfil the original mandate. They are gathering in spiritual families throughout the earth. He is giving the revelation of the foundational principles of Scriptures to them and bringing them to maturity under the leadership of fathers who know 'The Father'.

The message of the maturing of the saints is finding resonance among people who have longed for something more, being convinced that there had to be more to their church experience than what they were experiencing.

This book by Maurice Kennedy was a delightful surprise to me since I had only met him once on one of my trips to London. He has caught the essence of what the Spirit is saying to the Body of Christ in this hour. It is not only a book that brings spiritual understanding, it is also written in a very approachable style that comes with an invitation to journey into a discovery of these seminal principles. It is warm, welcoming and inviting without compromising the truth. I endorse this work without reservation and encourage the reader to consider engaging on this journey of discovering maturity and exact representation.

Dr Sam Soleyn.

Acknowledgements

I give thanks to Father God who by His grace provided me with a secure loving family in which I was raised. I am particularly grateful for the privilege of raising a family with my beautiful, loving wife Sharon Kennedy. It is through both the humanity and spirituality of my marriage to this gifted woman that this book has been birthed.

"He who finds a wife finds what is good and receives favour from the Lord." (Proverbs 18:22, NIV)

Sharon has supported me through the ups and downs of writing and has partnered with me in this project emotionally, intellectually and spiritually. A big thanks to our four adult children, Aharona, Asher, Hadassah, and Chaya who continually fill our home with love, laughter and warmth, creating an atmosphere that is conducive for creativity.

This book is a collection of thoughts downloaded into my spirit quite significantly over the last 20 years. What began earlier with some direct revelation through seed words from the Holy Spirit, has been watered and influenced significantly by numerous men and women of God. I believe it is important to acknowledge that although I am responsible for what I have written, my sources are much more extensive than the few names I am listing.

I received remotely the tutelage of the annual South African Apostolic School of Ministry ending in 2017 led by Thamo Naidoo and I have particularly been impacted by the ministry and works of Dr Sam Soleyn.

I wish to acknowledge men who are significant fathers to me: the late Wilfred Kennedy (my dad), late Rev Clifford

Fisher, late Rev Ron Brown, and the very present William Simpson (my father-in-law).

I want to also acknowledge the work of my editor Dr Jacqueline Samuels who has done her work with professionalism and has further served as a minister of Christ, prayerfully seeking God and adding grace to the project.

Introduction

> "*¹ In the past God spoke to our ancestors through the prophets at many times and in various ways, ² but in these last days He has spoken to us by His Son, whom He appointed heir of all things, and through whom also He made the universe. ³ The Son is the radiance of God's glory and the exact representation of His being, sustaining all things by His powerful Word.* (Hebrews 1:1-3, NIV)

Our relationship with Jesus the Christ is key to understanding the purpose of God the Father; by so doing we in turn understand our purpose in God. There is no knowing God outside His revelation of Himself. Jesus the Christ is Jehovah God's revelation of Himself. How indeed can one who is outside the realm of His creation fully reveal Himself to His creation?

I believe the book written to the Hebrews captures this. God starts building a physical stage for this unveiling through the creation of mankind in His own image, through the journey of a chosen people, through numerous prophets, priests, and kings, until finally the stage of earth is ready for His Eternal Son made flesh, Jesus the Christ.

Our intimacy with our Creator must be centred in God's final Word '*Son*'. We cannot make our own pathway, our own philosophy and hope to create an alternative to God's eternal plan. True wisdom is to receive in humility

God's revelation of Himself in *Son* and to explore this revelation through the

+navigation of the Holy Spirit.

This book **Son of Man, Son of God** is a contribution to that exploration. As I read these pages over and over again it is still incomplete; completion is to be achieved in your personal exploration even as I find completion in my continued exploration. If all you do is read the book, you will have hopefully achieved something, but my prayer is that you journey with the Holy Spirit into an intimacy of a Father-Son relationship in Christ.

This book began with a deeper revelation of my personal understanding of what it means to be a Christian. When we strip away culture and religiosity, when we get beyond pomp and ceremony, when we shed ourselves of qualifications and titles, we are left with a son of man who has been spiritually born again as a son of God. I intend to explore these references to Jesus as **Son of man, Son of God** in the Bible and consider how **Son of man, Son of God** applies to us as believers.

Maurice Kennedy

Chapter 1: How Can This Be?

"How can this be," Mary asked the angel, since I do not know a man?" (Luke 1:34; NKJV)

These were the words of Mary, when she was told by the angel Gabriel that she would have a child as a virgin. A very reasonable question that continues to resonate throughout the earth and indeed should do as we discuss the issue of Sonship. How can I be the mother of the Son of God? How can someone be Son of man and Son of God? How can divinity reside in humanity? How can this be? How does a female fit into Sonship?

How can one who is limited to time and space and subject to corporal drives such as hunger and thirst, also be a Son of the living God?

How can this be? I am God's son, His representative in the world, a leader in the church and yet as a man I struggle with my emotions when answers to my prayers are delayed with the natural unfolding of time. Darkness descends upon me.

The Holy Spirit can anoint me to deliver a powerful word in the morning and by the afternoon my being is gripped by doubt and despair. How can I be a Son of man, and also a Son of God? How can this be? How can these identities which sit at the opposing poles of a continuum reside together? *Son of man, Son of God* - How can this be?

Often the impossibility of the subject of our focus is due to the perspective from which we are viewing the situation. When we are faced with a particular challenging situation from our perspective we say: "*How could this be?*" God, from His perspective seeing the same situation without changing a thing says: "*This is how this is, and this is why this is*". What we need to do is ask the Holy Spirit to shift our paradigm to God's perspective. In other words what we need is revelation. Throughout this book I ask that you agree with my prayer for you to get revelation. Revelation can only be received by the Holy Spirit; information and knowledge is good, but it is not enough.

In reading this book you will get information and knowledge, yet it is far better to get revelation that leads to transformation. In the words of the Apostle Paul:

> "*[16] I have not stopped giving thanks for you, remembering you in my prayers. [17] I keep asking that the God of our Lord Jesus Christ, the glorious Father, may give you the Spirit of wisdom and revelation, so that you may know him better. [18] I pray that the eyes of your heart may be enlightened in order that you may know the hope to which he has called you, the riches of his glorious inheritance in his holy people, [19] and his incomparably great power for us who believe.*" (Ephesians 1:16-19; NIV)

How can this be? How can one be both Son of Man and Son of God? The impossibility with the subject of our focus is often due to the clash between mindset and language. We need to balance between our personal entrances into the Kingdom and the collective reality of the Kingdom. Unfortunately, the church tends to be plagued with a philosophy of individualism. We have a tendency to confuse our personal and individual entrance into the Kingdom through faith and repentance with the collective operation of the Kingdom.

While we enter the body of Christ individually, the body is a collective made of many parts, as the Apostle Paul notes in 1 Corinthians 12. With our individualistic philosophy, we have often interpreted Scripture through such a prism. In doing this we can interpret with the language of individualism when God is speaking the language of collectivism. The church is a body made up of many members. In the body of Christ there is no Sonship outside of Christ. There is one Son – Christ; in Him we are sons, as His collective body.

> "[26] *For ye are all the children of God by faith in Christ Jesus.* [27] *For as many of you as have been baptized into Christ have put on Christ.* [28] *There is neither Jew nor Greek, there is neither bond nor free, there is neither male nor female: for ye are all one in Christ Jesus.* [29] *And if ye be Christ's, then are ye Abraham's seed, and heirs according to the promise.* (Galatians 3: 26-29, NIV)

The idea of the church being an optional extra is as ludicrous as the idea of being a Son of God outside of Christ. How can this be? This will be the question that encapsulates all other questions as with this question, as a cup before the throne, we raise the content of this discussion, *Son of man, Son of God*, with a view to understanding the perspective of God.

The impossibility of a virgin having a child became totally simple. The Holy Spirit shall overshadow this young virgin and that which would have been otherwise impossible now becomes natural divine order. How can this be? It could be no other way.

Your REFLECTIONS

Mary asked, '*How could this be?*' What questions are you asking the Lord?

What practical steps can you take to prepare your mind to receive revelation from the Lord?

Chapter 2: My Genesis

"Very truly I tell you, no one can see the kingdom of God unless they are born again." (John 3: 3, NIV)

Becoming a Christian can be a releasing experience as one leaves an often-self-absorbed lifestyle to enter a Christ-centred life. It can mean, as in my case, a change of weekly schedule, a change of relationships, a change of direction and a change of ambition. For me the sky became bluer and the fields became a richer green. The Lord had done a work in my life that was a response to my faith but beyond my actions. His tangible grace moved in. Not only had He deposited something of Himself in me, He had also deposited me in Himself.

"For by grace through faith are you saved, it is the gift of God not of works so no one can boast." (Ephesians 2:8-9, NIV)

At the tender age of nineteen I was clueless to the ramifications of all this; however, His work of grace was real. As an infant in Christ I was dependent on my local church to navigate me in this journey; that is how I got immersed into Pentecostalism. I say this not as a negative, rather to acknowledge my journey. It is possible to exchange one world view for a better world view and still become lost. I found that my local church community, as does every community, had its own culture, its own way of doing things and as a youth and an impressionable infant in Christ, I simply flowed in the culture.

Great relationships in my life were established and many fundamental lessons learnt. However, it is important to recognise that culture, even a local church culture is not necessarily biblical. Jesus said a little yeast will change the whole loaf. Even though you have migrated from an unsaved community into a Christian community, its culture is still imperfect and therefore unreliable for an accurate definition of one's identity.

By my adopted church culture, I was told that I was a Christian saved by a great God and that I needed to walk in holiness. "Who am I?" "You are a Christian called out to walk in holiness" was the local church culture reply. The words were accurate but what was being modelled were a bunch of good people trying and hoping that they were living holy enough to make it into heaven. I exchanged my unsaved culture for this local church community culture.

I acknowledge that I am using my experience as a reference; your journey and your church culture may be totally different to mine. What I am sharing here is how migrating into a better community can still leave you somewhat lost because even a better community cannot define you.

We exert a lot of energy into trying to fit in. There appears to be a natural expectation from most groups, be it family, work, ethnic, friendship, religious, political, or educational, for its members to fit into a pre-assigned space. In these groups we can end up becoming what the group expects rather than growing into our uniquely designed whole.

The Jewish nation had their own predefined idea of the person, purpose and mission of the Messiah; because Jesus did not meet their specifications, He was rejected. The disciples also had their clear ideas of the Messiah's mission; as a result, the suggestion that this would involve dying was not well received. The pressure to be shaped into the image dictated by our peers is very real.

Hence the words of Romans 12:2a (The Voice): *"Do not allow this world to mold you in its own image. Instead, be transformed from the inside out by renewing your mind."*

Only our Heavenly Father can define us. It is the role of our Creator to give us definition of being and clarity of purpose.

The voice of the Father from heaven was God not only making a declaration of His relationship to Jesus, but as a Father critically giving Jesus definition. In these eternal words the Father encapsulated the boundaries of Jesus's person and a summary of His purpose.

"And lo a voice from heaven, saying, This is my beloved Son, in whom I am well pleased." (Matthew 3:17, KJV)

"While he yet spake, behold, a bright cloud overshadowed them: and behold a voice out of the cloud, which said, "This is my beloved Son, in whom I am well pleased; hear ye him." (Matthew 17:5, KJV)

To no other person in history has God intervened with His own voice to make such a personal declaration, which he did on two separate occasions: Jesus' baptism and His transfiguration. Jesus, uniquely is the only begotten Son, defined so by Father God. Jesus is not just another religious leader. He is not just another child of God. He is not just a model or pattern to be copied.

The notion of us being like Christ can only truly be actualised to the degree that we are in Christ. The deeper in Christ we progress, the more like Him we become, but we are not Him. He is the only human spirit that divides time and is actually defined as *Son*. He is the perfect visible representative of an invisible God. He is the fulfilment of God's plan, as it is in Him, that all who will be saved will be defined.

Jesus is the only human spirit qualified to contain all humanity. He is God poured out into humanity. Jesus is the revelation of Him who was hidden before time began and the culmination of the man seed Adam, who was sown at the beginning of time.

Your Reflections

Make notes about your spiritual journey and the major milestones in your journey.

Chapter 3: Who Am I?

"Who do people say the Son of Man is? Who do you say I am?" (Matthew 16:13, 15, NIV)

As a baby pushes its way through the darkness of the female birth canal into the light of the labour suite, so the human soul pushes forward through the internal fog of ignorance to apprehend the consciousness of personhood and purpose.

"Who am I?" is a question that links to an innate quest for self-discovery. The journey out of the womb is a physical type of the journey of the human soul that also begins in the darkness of the womb of ignorance with an inner compulsion to journey to and within the light of identity. Robert Ludlum's thrilling series of novels all based on the fictional character Jason Bourne seeking to discover his identity, has through the skill of writing managed to make millions by simply mirroring every person's story. This is the story that is readily identifiable by everyone who seeks to discover and live in their true identity while being challenged by opponents. These opponents are spirit assassins with the sole intention of thwarting this discovery and thus preventing our Creator's plan and purpose for our lives.

The question of identity resounds throughout the New Testament. More importantly, so too does the response to that question. Jesus in His famous discourse in Matthew's Gospel asks the questions:

Who do men say that I the Son of man am?

Who do you say that I am?

Why was Jesus asking such questions? The first thing to note is that He was not afraid of asking the question and secondly, the fact that He posed such a question emphasises its importance.

Did Jesus ask the questions out of a personal need for self-discovery? As Christian Bible students we might quickly respond "certainly not". However, I believe the question is worth some exploration. As questions of this nature are often rooted in a need to know. Could it be possible that Jesus in His human stage of development was seeking out from His peers some clarity of who He is and His purpose?

Is such a thought to be so quickly dismissed as irreverent and belittling of Him that we esteem as our Lord and Saviour? Could it be that in asking such questions that Jesus was also validating the resource of God's image in humanity? Let me not get ahead of myself, the question is this: Was Jesus on a journey of self-discovery or did He always know? Did He know before He asked the questions or did He ask the questions to know? If He asked the question to know does it lessen who He is?

My answer is definitely not - because He is who He is, but what it does is open our understanding. Jesus was not some fictitious character with enhanced powers. He was fully human, borne of a woman, which means as a baby He was like all babies fully dependent on His parents; if He did not get food He would die. He was initially non-verbal so He would cry for food just like other babies. He was dependent on His parents to change His diapers just like any other baby. Jesus was not pretending to be a baby, He was; His knowledge and abilities were limited to His stage of development. Jesus learnt and developed from the input from those around Him.

What I am saying is that this, if anything, magnifies the miracle of the incarnation of how a God without limits could pour Himself into humanity and in so doing limit Himself to time and space. That means He made Himself dependent on the passage of time for physical, mental, and spiritual development. In other words, Jesus had to discover Himself physically, mentally and spiritually.

So whether this discourse was about His personal self-discovery or solely about the development of His disciples, it is important to note that Jesus was also learning and discovering.

The Bible describes Jesus as one that was growing in grace and truth:

"And the child grew and became strong; he was filled with wisdom, and the grace of God was on him." (Luke 2:40, NIV)

"And Jesus grew in wisdom and stature, and in favour with God and man." (Luke 2:52, NIV)

This suggests that Jesus was subjected to the rules of humanity; the living God confined Himself to time and space. He had to grow.

Jesus had to be educated. In this He modelled a learning style that was spirit led and not just led by the soul. While there was lots of information, Jesus was seeking revelation.

Even through His peers He sought out the undertones of the Father's voice, *he who has ears to hear let him hear.*

Jesus asked the question, *"Who do they say that I the Son of man am?"* There were lots of responses with much information. Right now, in our modern world there is more information than ever. With technological advancement we literally have a tsunami of information. More books are being written than ever before with the birth of eBooks and at the touch of a button we can get pages of responses to almost any inquiry. Jesus was not impressed by the responses, which led Him to ask a further question, *"Who do you say that I am?"* (Matthew 16:15, ESV) In Peter's response Jesus heard the undertones of the voice of His Father: *"You are the Christ, the Son of the living God"*. (Matthew 16:16, ESV)

As you sift through the information presented in this book do not just hear with your soul, hear with your spirit; listen for the undertones of the Father's voice, and seek out revelation. Read a section more than once, search the Scriptures for yourself, leave, pray, and then return. Please do not confine this reading to just a conversation between you and these pages. It is imperative that you have conversations with the Father.

> *"9 So I say to you: Ask and it will be given to you; seek and you will find; knock and the door will be opened to you. 10 For everyone who asks receives; the one who seeks finds; and to the*

one who knocks, the door will be opened." (Luke 11:9-10, NIV)

Jesus needed revelation to make the transition into purpose and full consciousness of personhood. If Jesus needed revelation, how much more do we?

Jesus replied, *"Blessed are you, Simon son of Jonah, for this was not revealed to you by flesh and blood, but by my Father in heaven."* (Matthew 16:17, NIV)

One of the many notable facts of the Matthew 16 discourse is that within it Jesus accepts the title of *Son of man* and the title of *Son of God*. One title accepting His absolute humanity, the other His absolute divinity.

Your REFLECTIONS

How are you responding to the thirst for God in your life?

How have you discovered your identity so far?

Chapter 4: Why Son?

"The Son is the radiance of God's glory and the exact representation of his being, sustaining all things by his powerful word." (Hebrews 1:3, NIV)

Before even considering the titles '*Son of God*' or '*Son of man*', let us first consider the description: *son*. Why would God even choose the term son as opposed to any other description? Why not daughter, cousin, brother, sister, uncle… etc? God is very deliberate and purposeful. Let us not be afraid to bring our very basic questions to God. It is not irreverent. If He is God, it makes absolute sense to go directly to Him who is the source of everything with our questions. Our heavenly Father takes pleasure in responding to His children. Note however that our receiving of those responses is subject to time and space; it is not always as immediate as we would like.

So why '*Son*'? Let us deconstruct so we can reconstruct. 'Son' is the male description for the offspring of man as opposed to the daughter; it is the seed producing offspring and in that seed is the DNA of the male family line. There is no family line without seed. This is a fundamental principle of all living things. In the human family this does not make the son more important than a daughter. What we have are simply two offspring with two different functions. The male offspring son produces seed that fertilises the egg; the female offspring daughter incubates seed and gives birth to a child thus extending the family line. Both contribute to the genetic makeup, the DNA of the child. Both are essential to the purpose of God, and in both is the image of God.

"So God created mankind in His own image, in the image of God He created them; male and female He created them." (Genesis 1:27, NIV)

God deliberately and purposefully chose the term 'son' because in accordance with the law of all living things, the son produces the seed. Therefore, the term 'son' becomes a generic term for seed producer or carrier, spiritually applied to male and female.

"There is neither Jew nor Gentile, neither slave nor free, nor is there male and female, for you are all one in Christ Jesus." (Galatians 3:28, NIV)

This is not to suggest that gender is not important but rather that the use of the term 'son' spiritually applies to both men and women in Christ. We carry and produce the life producing seed of God in Christ. When we are located in Christ then we are and can only be the son of God. For we are assembled in Him as His body. When God the Father looks over us, He sees Christ His beloved Son.

We need to go still further in the purpose of God's deliberate selection of the terminology 'son', because the selection of son is a vital complement to the selection of the term 'father', as the 'son' is then the image of the father, identified as an exact representation.

In order to enable our appreciation and understanding of the selection of 'son' we need to also deconstruct and reconstruct the selection of the term 'father' to further unearth why Son is chosen as a compliment. It is also important to note that God also specifically selected the son who was firstborn, which has a particular cultural significance in terms of inheritance and representation in the chosen culture of the Jews in which again God deliberately and purposefully chose to incarnate Himself. The firstborn son is entitled to a double portion of inheritance as an heir and is the most honoured representative of his father.

Hebrews Chapter 1

> "1 *In the past God spoke to our ancestors through the prophets at many times and in various ways, 2 but in these last days he has spoken to us by his Son, whom he appointed heir of all things, and through whom also he made the universe. 3 The Son is the radiance of God's glory and the exact representation of his being, sustaining all things by his powerful word. After he had provided purification for sins, he sat down at the right hand of the Majesty in heaven. 4 So he became as much superior to the angels as the name he has inherited is superior to theirs. 5 For to which of the angels did God ever say, "You are my Son; today I have become your Father"? Or again, "I will be his Father, and he will be my Son"? 6 And again, when God brings his firstborn into the world, he says, "Let all God's angels worship him. 7 "In speaking of the angels he says, "He makes his angels spirits, and his servants flames of fire. 8 "But about the Son he says, "Your throne, O God, will last for*

ever and ever; a scepter of justice will be the scepter of your kingdom. 9 You have loved righteousness and hated wickedness; therefore God, your God, has set you above your companions by anointing you with the oil of joy. 10 "He also says, "In the beginning, Lord, you laid the foundations of the earth, and the heavens are the work of your hands. 11 They will perish, but you remain; they will all wear out like a garment. 12 You will roll them up like a robe; like a garment they will be changed. But you remain the same, and your years will never end. 13 "To which of the angels did God ever say, "Sit at my right hand until I make your enemies a footstool for your feet"? 14 Are not all angels ministering spirits sent to serve those who will inherit salvation? (Hebrews 1:1-14, NIV)

Your REFLECTIONS

What are your thoughts on 'why son' as you read Hebrews Chapter one?

Chapter 5: Why Father?

"Our Father in heaven, hallowed be your name".
(Matthew 6:9, NIV)

As previously stated, God is deliberate and purposeful. He is perfect in knowledge as He is not bound by the limitations of time and space. He is the only *forever* and *always* being so He acts according to His knowledge. As His knowledge is perfect and complete, all His actions are then deliberate and purposeful as He knows the end from the beginning.

Words are undoubtedly important as they are containers carrying meaning. They carry meaning between humans and they carry meaning between God and humans. Words are vessels of the spirit, hence Jesus was able to say 'the words I speak are spirit and life' (John 6:63); therefore God's choice of terminology is important.

God has chosen very male orientated terminology to reveal Himself. For some this could be a stumbling block, while others might not resonate well with God choosing the Jews and not another nation.

However, rather than dismiss God as racist or sexist, it would be more appropriate to approach God with a 'why?', so that we might hear what He is communicating to us. Let him that is willing hear! If everyone simply recreates God in their own prejudices we are left with a world of hate and division.

So why 'father'? Is another important query in order to further appreciate why 'son'?

'Father' as a term speaks of source, leader, provision and protection. The father is the progenitor of the seed. It is a relational term for it is out of the very loins of the father that life and family are formed. The 'father' then ensures that his family is protected and provided for as it grows and develops. The key thing about this term is that it has no existence or purpose outside of relationship.

The female equivalent term is not less important, but He chose the male term to convey a particular message. God is bound to use language that best reveals Himself to us, but He is not male man or female man; He is God. God transcends gender. The male term is used to communicate meaning and not to limit being. The term *'Father'* tells us that God has always been a God of relationship and that this relationship pre-existed before creation within God: Father, Son, and Holy Spirit. It also informs us that it is out of this invisible realm of relationship that God the Father has created a visible, physical realm of relationships.

The Apostle John's theology can be reduced to six key words: "*God is Spirit*" and "*God is love*". As we explore God's choice of the term *'Father'* we see that it synchronises with the theology of John to present a God who is an invisible Spirit motivated by love, who has chosen to share Himself in a visible and physical realm. God as a *'Father'* has created the physical realm because of His love. The depth if His love is exemplified in John 3:16 as again the Apostle John captures the heart of a Father in a few choice words:

"For God so loved the world (physical realm) that He gave, (released, sacrificed, emptied) Himself through His only Son that whosoever believes in Him should not perish but shall have eternal life" (John 3:16) (but be made a citizen of the Kingdom of God or a member of the family of God. (*Interpretation in brackets mine*).

The relational factor of the term Father is key to its selection. The Word reveals a God who is plural and who in His plurality is love. You can be a man without having children, but you cannot be a father without offspring. Father speaks of plurality. We know that there is another description of this offspring: the Word.

'*Word*' speaks of an intimate relationship flowing from the core of the speaker. There is no speaker without word and there is no word without a speaker.

> *"1 In the beginning [before all time] was the Word (Christ), and the Word was with God, and the Word was God Himself. 2 He was [continually existing] in the beginning [co-eternally] with God. 3 All things were made and came into existence through Him; and without Him not even one thing was made that has come into being. 13 who were born, not of blood [natural conception], nor of the will of the flesh [physical impulse], nor of the will of man [that of a natural father], but of God [that is, a divine and supernatural birth—they are born of God—spiritually transformed, renewed, sanctified]. 14 And the Word (Christ) became flesh, and lived among us; and we [actually] saw His glory, glory as belongs to the [One and] only begotten Son of the Father, [the Son who is truly unique, the only One of His*

> *kind, who is] full of grace and truth (absolutely free of deception)."* (John 1:1-3, 13-14; AMP)

In keeping with the choice of '*Father*', what better and more appropriate description for the eternal offspring of the father than '*Son*'. It complements like for like, the *Son* is the exact representation of the Father.

God is an eternal Father. His eternal Fatherhood is dependent on Him having an eternal offspring. This eternal offspring in keeping with the meaning and choice of Father can best be described as Son.

Your REFLECTIONS

What does 'Father' mean to you?

Chapter 6: Jesus Son of Man?

> *"For this reason he had to be made like them, fully human in every way, in order that he might become a merciful and faithful high priest in service to God, and that he might make atonement for the sins of the people."* (Hebrews 2:17, NIV)

Generally, biblical hermeneutics informs us that the title *'son of man'*, when used in reference to Jesus speaks of His humanity, while the title *'Son of God'*, when used in reference to Jesus, speaks of His divinity. However, when the usage of these terms are explored in context, such a clear demarcation in usage is not completely evident. Once again, we often de-construct for the sake of study, but then fail to see the subject of focus as the whole that it is. Just because there are different elements to our make-up does not mean that the whole is not greater than the sum of the parts. We are made of body, soul and spirit but somehow when God formed us of these separate elements, something greater than simply the sum of these parts was created: *"man the image of God"*. Hopefully as we explore the Word together and we consider the shades of meaning in the elements, our focus will be primarily on the whole as revealed by the Holy Spirit.

'Son of man' is used eighty-eight times in the New Testament in reference to Jesus. It is the title Jesus mostly uses in reference to Himself with the simple

meaning of His membership as part of the human race. Within this title there is also an echo of its usage in Daniel 7: 13-14. In this passage there is a prophetic reference to a specific human being, a Messianic King who is sent by God from heaven as the reigning King to usher in the Kingdom of God on earth. The fact that He is born of flesh does not change His status. He is the eternal King of kings clothed in flesh. His infancy, His human development from baby to man does not change the truth of His identity. In fact, it only amplifies the miracle of *Emmanuel God with us*. The title '*son of man*' therefore speaks of His humanity; it is also an echo of a particular prophesied King, the Messiah.

> "*In my vision at night I looked, and there before me was one like a son of man, coming with the clouds of heaven. He approached the Ancient of Days and was led into his presence. He was given authority, glory and sovereign power; all nations and peoples of every language worshiped him. His dominion is an everlasting dominion that will not pass away, and his kingdom is one that will never be destroyed.*"
> (Daniel, 7:13-14, NIV)

The much-used title *Son of man* can be seen as an acknowledgement and celebration of Jesus' humanity. God called the prophet Ezekiel "*son of man*" ninety-three times. God was simply calling Ezekiel a human being, which in itself is fundamental to our salvation. 1 John 4:2 tells us, "*This is how you can recognize the Spirit of God: Every spirit that acknowledges that Jesus Christ has come in the flesh is from God.*" (NIV)

The humanity of Jesus is not an optional extra in terms of Christian doctrine, it is fundamental to our faith. But the title '*Son of man*' must also be seen within the cultural Jewish context of the community in which He was born in which it was a direct reference to a specific member of humanity, the Messiah.

> *"Day after day, in the temple courts and from house to house, they never stopped teaching and proclaiming the good news that Jesus is the Messiah."* (Acts 5:42, NIV)

When we hear '*son of man*' with our 21st century non-Jewish mind-set, we hear 'human being', but when the Jews, who were eagerly awaiting the promised One, heard that title, they would undoubtedly have heard a Messianic reference. Although there is an innate reference in this title to Jesus's humanity, '*son of man*' is also a clear Messianic claim. He is the King of kings whose reign will have no end. His total humanity is essential to his Messianic identity.

> *"Then the seventh angel sounded [his trumpet]; and there were loud voices in heaven, saying, "The kingdom (dominion, rule) of the world has become the kingdom of our Lord and of His Christ; and He will reign forever and ever."* (Revelation 11:15, AMP)

Your REFLECTIONS

What does Jesus being 'fully human' mean to you?

Chapter 7: Jesus Son of God?

"In the beginning was the Word, and the Word was with God, and the Word was God." (John 1:1, NIV)

'Son of God', when applied to Jesus in the Bible tends to reference His divinity. Yet it is important to note that in the Bible it is not only used to describe Jesus but also more widely regarding those in some special relationship with God. The term is used in reference to angels, kings, and other chosen followers. Furthermore, when this title is used in reference to Jesus, it also has a messianic significance and is not always strictly speaking of His divinity in the context of the Scripture.

As stated in the previous chapter, this understanding is significant, lest we simply see the titles *Son of God* and *Son of man* as polarised opposites rather than roles that can exist in synergy. In study we naturally deconstruct but this does not mean that the whole is not greater than the deconstructed parts. The whole is not always just a sum of its parts, it has a unique identity of its own. Sometimes in our dismantling to understand, we can lose sight of that unique identity.

It is noteworthy to acknowledge that sin has corrupted every dimension of our humanity by creating a disconnect between us and God, causing even our way of learning to be challenged. The greatest mind without the navigation of the Holy Spirit is at best flawed.

I have worked in the field of learning difficulties and disabilities for over 25 years and now I must conclude that without the Holy Spirit our learning abilities are severely impaired; in this sense we all have learning difficulties. Since the human mind in isolation of the Holy Spirit cannot be trusted, we must all come humbly to the throne of God knowing that this gift of intellect can only be trusted as it is led by the Holy Spirit.

However, it is still true that '*Son of God*' speaks of the pre-existent relationship within God: between God the Father and the person otherwise known as the Word. The relationship within God defines all future relationships with God. It is a relationship of total intimacy, one of true oneness. By this relationship all other relationships are measured and are the standard or rule of relationship. Herein is a relationship of pure equality. The only other person that shares eternally in this equality in God is the Holy Spirit and even then His role is to reveal this standard of relationship to the creation and cause order to come through the express standard of this father and son relationship. The Father speaks, the Son is His perfect expression and the Holy Spirit implements.

Being in His very nature God, equality with God was an unnecessary pursuit because He was equal. (Philippians 2: 6)

This is the premier relationship. We do not define God, rather it is God out of this relationship that defines us. In this relationship is encapsulated the entire plan and purpose of God. The lesser cannot give definition to the greater as it is the greater that contains the lesser.

This title when ascribed to Jesus is different to its other usage; it is unquestionably in this context a claim to divinity. This title cannot be separated from the Messianic title '*Son of Man*'. Hence when used this title of Jesus is either total blasphemy or the most glorious truth. There is no middle ground... He cannot be just a good man or one of the Prophets....He is either divine or the worst deceiver. He is either the Christ or the anti-Christ.

Son of God, Son of man is the revelation of Jesus of Nazareth being the most glorious truth. In these titles we see that He is the perfect expression of the Father. He is one with the Father....*I and my Father are one.* This is not just an honorary title; He is the Eternal Word made flesh. ...it is in this sense that He is *the only begotten Son of God* and thus also the Messianic '*Son of man*'.

"*And who do you say that I am? ...You are the Christ the Son of the living God.*" (Matthew 16:15-16, NLV)

In reference to Jesus there is a unique usage of the terms '*Son of God/ Son of man*'; when combined in this unique usage we have an undeniable declaration of God incarnated.

Just like '*Son of man*' is used in the Bible as a synonym for human being, so too does '*Son of God*' have a generic usage in the Bible referring to beings created in the image of God. But be clear, the Scripture is very definitive, Jesus is not just another created being. In His conception, to highlight the fact that He was direct from the heavens, there was no man involved, rather He was conceived in a virgin by the Holy Spirit. This was as unique an entry as Adam, however the lineage of Adam was bypassed so that none could say that Jesus was born in sin and shaped in iniquity from Adam's lineage. Jesus was born of a woman since He had to be fully human, but unlike anyone else He was God poured out into humanity.

> *"But emptied Himself [without renouncing or diminishing His deity, but only temporarily giving up the outward expression of divine equality and His rightful dignity] by assuming the form of a bond-servant, and being made in the likeness of men [He became completely human but was without sin, being fully God and fully man]."* (Philippians 2:7, AMP)

In becoming flesh Jesus laid aside His glory and subjected Himself to the limitation of time and space like any other created being. It is clear from followers and opposers, that Jesus was not just identifying as one of the many children of God, rather as the eternal Son of God who became flesh. For His antagonists the response of His claim is the foundation of their accusation and their demands for crucifixion.

All roads in history reach their destination with the emergence of the firstborn Son of God. This was never just some rescue operation; this was a deliberate and purposed act of God. The Word was waiting to be revealed in the clothing of humanity from before the beginning of time. While Adam and Abraham were on the stage of life, Jesus was waiting backstage by the curtains for the fullness of time, for *"before Abraham was, I am."* (John 8:58, NIV).

When these terms '*Son of God*' and '*Son of man*' are used in relation to Jesus, they are not merely generically referring to His human status or His being one of many children of God. <u>He is the only begotten Son of God and He is the messianic Son of Man</u>. He is the firstborn. In Jesus heaven has finally arrived on earth. He is fully God and fully man. He is the only one qualified to create a passage to heaven even as He had made a passage from heaven to earth. Jesus was not waiting for Adam to fall; Adam's disobedience was factored into the plan of God. God had the solution before the problem; God had the answer before the question; God knew the end before the beginning.

The idea of the greater containing the lesser is a theme that runs throughout creation; the universe contains planets; planets-notably earth where we dwell-contains waters and continents; continents contain countries and countries then contain other divisions, and so on. The greater always contains the lesser, hence the only one able to contain creation is the Creator.

Therefore, it is in this eternal relationship of Father, Son, and Holy Spirit that sits all the plans and purposes of God. Jesus did not just come to save us from our sins but rather to make Himself a spiritual container where all who receive His grace and truth can also engage with God as Father in Him. There only needs to be one Son who poured His divinity into humanity. He did so knowing that as a human spirit being He would be large enough to receive the 'whosoever believes' of John 3: 16. He has the capacity to contain everyone that receives the Holy Spirit. Therefore, we who are in Christ are able to share in His Sonship. As by the one man death entered the world, so too by the one man shall all be saved.

> "*15 But not as the offence, so also is the free gift. For if through the offence of one many be dead, much more the grace of God, and the gift by grace, which is by one man, Jesus Christ, hath abounded unto many. 16 And not as it was by one that sinned, so is the gift: for the judgment was by one to condemnation, but the free gift is of many offences unto justification. 17 For if by one man's offence death reigned by one; much more they which receive abundance of grace and of the gift of righteousness shall reign in life by one, Jesus Christ.) 18 Therefore as by the offence of one judgment came upon all men to condemnation; even so by the righteousness of one the free gift came upon all men unto justification of life. 19 For as by one man's disobedience many were made sinners, so by the obedience of one shall many be made righteous.* (Romans 5:15-19, KJV)

The church then is rightly described as the body of Christ. It is only as we are fitted together in Him that we have definition, meaning and purpose.

Your REFLECTIONS

What is so special about Jesus's status as the Son of God?

Chapter 8: A Sacred Moment

> "*Father, I want those you have given me to be with me where I am, and to see my glory, the glory you have given me because you loved me before the creation of the world.*" (John 17: 24, NIV)

There are so many passages that exemplify the intimacy of this relationship; one that I choose to give particular focus is Jesus' prayer in John 17. Here we do not just see the Father's heart or the Son's heart. Instead, what He has allowed us to see is the intimate interaction between the two. This prayer is a window into the heart of the perfect Father and Son relationship, giving us the privilege to enter and engage our five senses in the machinations of this eternal relationship.

This is not just Jesus doing a pastoral prayer for His followers, although that in itself is a showstopper. This is Jesus saying, '*taste, smell, feel, see, and hear what my relationship is like with my Father.*' We enter this revelation as our spirit is led by His Spirit; but then our five senses are engaged in the revelation as God's Word is earthed within us. This is not just a moment to be observed, but to be experienced.

To witness real personal interaction between mankind and God is to encounter a truly sacred moment. We are not speaking of a religious interaction, Christian or otherwise. When a man or a woman is truly engaged in prayer and worship, then there is a heavenly visitation to earth even as there is an earthly visitation to heaven. It is indeed holy ground.

Jesus allows us several windows into these sacred moments in His life. In fact, the reality is that the whole life of Jesus as witnessed in the Bible is one complete sacred moment because He is a living testimony of one who prays without ceasing. However, to hold this in the limitations of a physical realm we need to break things down into chapter and verse. To capture this truth, we in our limitation need to focus on one frame. In doing this it would give us theological balance to remember that Jesus lived the sacred life.

> [1] *After Jesus said this, he looked toward heaven and prayed: "Father, the hour has come. Glorify your Son, that your Son may glorify you.* [2] *For you granted him authority over all people that he might give eternal life to all those you have given him.* [3] *Now this is eternal life: that they know you, the only true God, and Jesus Christ, whom you have sent.* [4] *I have brought you glory on earth by finishing the work you gave me to do.* [5] *And now, Father, glorify me in your presence with the glory I had with you before the world began.* (John 17: 1-5, NIV)

John 17 starts with how Jesus begins His prayer: Turning His eyes to heaven is simply and clearly stating that this spiritual communication had His complete attention. His whole being was poised for spirit to Spirit communication, as simple and natural and as fast as that is. Our innate ability to do this is an often unrecognised and unappreciated gift from our Creator.

We are the only earth beings who have been created with spiritual properties so that we, within fractions of seconds literally dividing time, can connect with the eternal. *"He turned his eyes towards heaven"*. The simple fact that we are created in His image means that we are able to position ourselves for communication with our Creator.

In a physical sense whether this is with our eyes opened and turned to the skies or with our heads bowed and our eyes closed, this is immaterial, what matters is that spiritually our being has been poised for connecting with our Creator.

Jesus's opening words then frame His prayer: He addresses God as *'Father'* and He acknowledges His Sonship. This is not just a prayer about relationship, it is a prayer of relationship, a relationship of the highest order; a Son begotten of the Father, bearing His image.

In this prayer Jesus employs the full status of this relationship: He speaks of glory and being glorified, He not only stands in His status as the Son of Man but also as the eternal Son of God, there is no shying away from His identity. He openly and unabashedly embraces who He is; that is fundamental to His dialogue with His Father.

In Jesus' approach we see total respect and a sense of equality as He goes before His Father as both a creature of the earth and a member of the eternal Godhead at the same time.

It exemplifies the statement of one who, being in the form of God, thought it not robbery to be equal with God.

(Philippians 2: 6). Here we see humility demonstrated as Jesus balances His approach between creature and Creator...between servant and King...God clothed in flesh: **Son of man, Son of God**.

The Son's glory is directly linked to His purpose of being an exact representation of His Father in the physical realm; in this the Father is glorified. The purpose of the Son is to glorify the Father and He fulfils this purpose by receiving His glory as the pre-existent Son from His Father. The Father who has not laid aside His glory is the only one qualified to confirm and define the status of the Son. This is done through a glory transfer.

It is important to note that the Son's identity is defined by the Father... Hence we hear the voice of the Father resonating on more than one occasion "*This is my beloved Son...*". Just like in an earthly kingdom we see a crown given to a prince from a king, so also do we see the Father commuting His glory to His Son.

John 17 verses 1 to 5 is all about the necessary flow of this glory from Father to Son and from Son to Father. This flow of glory is orchestrated by the Holy Spirit. That which was only accessible pre-creation in God, is now through God made flesh, flowing between the spiritual realm and the physical realm.

"*There is a river whose streams make glad the city of God.* (Hebrews 1:6, NIV) There is a flow between the invisible and the visible. God has achieved the impossible. He has made His glory accessible to another dimension. Let us take a moment to bask in this dynamic flow of glory between Father and Son. This flow of glory is not just some fantastic occurrence that is external to

God, it is God and that is why He has achieved the impossible. He has brought His Triune invisible self into the physical world and in this prayer, Jesus drew back the curtain to give us a glimpse of the glorious dynamic of the relationship within God.

If this is not glorious enough, this flow of glory which we are getting a glimpse of in John 17, was set to become the believer's direct point of access to God within God; it is a pathway between realms. In other words, this flow of glory doubles up as the believer's private executive route between heaven and earth. We shall pursue this thought further in subsequent chapters.

John 17 verses 1 to 5 is the platform upon which the entire prayer between Father and Son is communicated. It is the private executive channel reserved for Godhead communications. Besides praying for His present disciples, Jesus actually prays for us His future disciples, that we might also access this private executive channel reserved for the Godhead. Our passport into this channel is our use of the name of Jesus, not just as some magic formulae at the end of a prayer. We can only truly access this channel by taking on the identity of Christ; the Apostle Paul describes it as being "in Christ".

The core reason for the existence of the physical realm is that it would be a conduit of this flow of glory and here in this sacred moment Jesus draws open the curtain and reveals the Holy of Holies: His relationship with His heavenly Father as never seen before. The invisible is made visible, heaven has come to earth.

Capture this moment with the camera of your spirit: a river of glory flowing freely within God from Father to Son and from Son to Father, unrestricted anointing, pure beauty, absolute power, perfect oneness. Then hear again the eternal words of the psalmist:

> *"There is a river whose streams make glad the city of God, the holy place where the Most High dwells."* (Psalm 46: 4, NIV)

Behold! This is not just another son in prayer: this is God revealed: Father, Son and Holy Spirit. It is impossible to know God outside His methodology of revelation. The revelation that is *Son* is intended to catapult us into the secret workings of God.

I would strongly suggest that you read this chapter again as you read alongside several times the full prayer of Jesus in John 17, that you might capture the revelation of the inner dynamic of the relationship within God, glory flowing between Father and Son orchestrated by the Holy Spirit.

In this moment in time God has achieved the impossible. He has opened up His previously located spiritual sanctum to descend into the physical dimension. Like Joshua, command time to pause as you immerse yourself in the flow of glory within God, experiencing with your whole being, this opening of heaven on earth.

This is a sacred moment.

Your REFLECTIONS

As you have your 'sacred moment', make notes here of the thoughts and pictures that the Holy Spirit is sharing with you?

Chapter 9: Only Begotten Son

> *"No man hath seen God at any time, the only begotten Son, which is in the bosom of the Father, he hath declared him."* (John 1:18, KJV) *And again, when God brings his firstborn into the world, he says, "Let all God's angels worship him."* (Hebrews 1:6, NIV)

It is really important to understand what is meant by *first born* and *only begotten*; Jesus the Son of man needed to know this. He needed to know His identity and purpose and there was none qualified on earth to perform that function. Again, in this revelation of relationship in John 17 we see Jesus clearly stipulating that He has been given His identity by His Heavenly Father. In both verse eleven and twelve Jesus repeats the phrase "*the name you gave me*". The only one qualified to define the Son in heaven and earth is the Holy Father. Joseph is not qualified, Mary is not qualified, the religious leaders are not qualified, the political leaders are not qualified, even the crowd representing democracy is not qualified.

The only one able to truly define or clarify the boundaries of this being Jesus is the One who sits outside the boundaries of time and is able to comprehend the full impact of this person: past, present and future. If Jesus was relying on democracy, which we in western societies almost hold as infallible, He would have been a King one day and a blasphemer the next day.

Democracy, although one of the more equitable systems compared to other sinful systems, is not infallible and certainly does not have the capacity to define that which it has not created and in fact is the source of all creation. Democracy is also representative of the crowd which always seeks to fit subjects of its focus into pre-created spaces.

I hear echoes of Romans 12 where Paul encourages us not to be squashed into images or identities made by the world, but rather to be liberated by a continuously renewed mind. It is even suggested that Judas was trying to force the hand of Jesus to fit into the Jewish nationalistic expectation as the revolutionist. Although Democracy might be fairer than other systems, it is also fickle. We see this in the massive swings from political right to left and left to right in terms of modern-day voting patterns. The crowds of Jerusalem demonstrated this as they went from 'hail him' to 'kill him' within a week.

While crowds, community leaders, church leaders, and family can give us valuable insight, the only reliable definer of our identity is our Heavenly Father. Jesus said, *"the name you gave me"*; the understanding of His identity was founded in His Holy Father. It is important to understand that when Jesus spoke of 'name' in this context it is much more than a sound used to attract our attention. He is referring to His unchanging eternal relationship with God and His purpose of being. In fact, Jesus specifically states in these verses that the Name of God is the Name which He has been given.

"Holy Father, protect them by the power of your name, the name you gave me, so that they may be one as we are one." (John 17: 11, NIV)

His shared name with the Father makes Him one with the Father in terms of relationship and purpose of being. This again confirms the unique reality of Jesus the Christ, since like no other He is both God and man. Jesus is the only begotten in the sense that He alone is the only pre-existent Son who always was and forever will be. He is the Eternal Word that forever was God and is God.

Jesus therefore was the only one that could be begotten as God because He is God. In other words, Jesus like no other is exact in His representation of God. *"The Son is the radiance of God's glory and the exact representation of His being, sustaining all things by His powerful word."* Hebrews 1:3, BSB). He alone is entitled because He is God made flesh. (Philippians 2: 6-11). That is why there is no other name under heaven and earth by which we might be saved.

What about Adam? Adam in all his privileges as an image bearer did not and could not hold such a position. He was created directly by God as a son of God. However, like Esau, by his disobedience Adam relinquished that birthright and became dead in sin, leaving the only one righteous Son, the only begotten Son, Jesus the Christ. Even Adam can only be redeemed through faith in Jesus the Christ.

"For there is one mediator between God and man and that is the man Christ Jesus." (1 Timothy 2: 5, NIV)

If Adam or his lineage could have been saved in any other way, then Christ's death would have been for nothing. It is important to clarify as fundamental to our understanding of divine Sonship that Jesus is uniquely and distinctively the only begotten Son of God and that there is no Sonship outside of Jesus the Christ. Our claim to Sonship only has its legitimacy based on our own relational position in Christ Jesus. The idea of being a son and having no relationship with Christ is as ridiculous as claiming Christianity and yet being a committed follower of another religion. We are sons only in Him. Outside of Him there is no Sonship. We need to be baptised into His body by the Holy Spirit and we need the Holy Spirit to be in us. The integrity of our Sonship is founded in a real continuous relationship in Christ. There is no father-son relationship with God outside of Christ. Jesus the Christ is the only begotten Son of God and we can address God as Father only in Him.

Jesus answered, "I am the way and the truth and the life. No one comes to the Father except through me." (John 14: 6, NIV)

Jesus is also the firstborn Son. In addition to Jesus being the only Son, He must be before Adam.

> *Also to enlighten all men* and *make plain to them what is the plan [regarding the Gentiles and providing for the salvation of all men] of the mystery kept hidden through the ages* and *concealed until now in [the mind of] God Who created all things by* Christ Jesus. (Ephesians 3:9, AMPC)

God is not reactionary; the solution must be before the problem. Therefore, the presence of an eternal Father demands the presence of an eternal Son. He was there with God in the beginning because He is God. (John 1: 1). Only God could be with God in the beginning because in the beginning was God (Genesis 1: 1) and only the divine Word qualifies. *"And the Word became flesh and dwelt among us."* (John 1: 14, NIV)

When Jesus was challenged regarding His greatness in comparison to Abraham, He responded by saying *"Before Abraham was, I am"* (John 8:58, ESV). Of course, 'I am' is a clear reference to the identified Name of God as presented to Moses. He is the eternal Son; if the question was asked regarding Adam, Jesus could have answered with the same clarity "before Adam was, I am". Jesus has no beginning and no end. It should be noted then that the concept of *firstborn* in reference to Christ goes beyond the limitations of chronology as He was before time.

The firstborn son by virtue of his position in the Jewish family is entitled to a double portion of his father's estate, meaning that he was entitled to the main portion of the father's estate. Jesus as the firstborn goes even further. He said, *"I and the Father are one"* (John 10:30, NASB 1995) therefore all that belongs to the Father belongs to the Son. Jesus can rightly say this because He is not only the firstborn heir, He is the only Son and thus the only heir. Thoughts of being Jesus's younger siblings might engender warm and fuzzy feelings. They however carry hermeneutical inaccuracy if we begin to perceive ourselves as being sons independent of Christ, as we are only sons in Christ.

The firstborn son is the most honoured and exact representative of the father. Unlike any other, the firstborn son carries the likeness of the father in terms of power and purpose. He is the father's ideal representative in that he perfectly reflects the image of his father. Our Sonship only exists in Christ as our Sonship and Christ's Sonship are one and the same.

We therefore share in His inheritance as a firstborn. We are joint heirs with Jesus. Jesus the Christ needs to be understood as the spiritual ark that is able to contain all those that would be saved, and this ark is the ark of Sonship. The ark of Noah that preserved humanity through the righteous judgement of God is but a type and shadow of Jesus the Christ, who is the true ark of deliverance and redemption. Jesus the Christ is therefore rightly the firstborn of many sons.

Let me summarise it this way: God has in human history only had two sons: Jesus and Adam. Jesus was always first. Adam, however, was first revealed on the stage of human history while Jesus awaited in the wings of human history for the fullness of time. It is important to note that Jesus was not just hanging around waiting on time to pass; rather He was with the Father in equal reign and governance as God in eternity.

Adam forsook his Sonship by becoming dead in sin through disobedience, leaving only Jesus as the Son who remained obedient. We are either seen in Adam, as dead in sin and shaped in iniquity or we are seen in Jesus as Son.

Your REFLECTIONS

Why is Jesus the **only begotten** Son?

Why is Jesus the **first-born** Son?

Chapter 10: Another Genesis

> *"I came from the Father and entered the world; now I am leaving the world and going back to the Father."* (John 16:28, NIV)

It is by no coincidence that the globally recognised calendar is centred on the person of Christ. He uniquely divided time and caused the count to begin again. Jesus and not Adam is the Lord of time, He literally created another Genesis.

> *"1 In the beginning was the Word, and the Word was with God, and the Word was God. 2 He was with God in the beginning. 3 Through him all things were made; without him nothing was made that has been made. 4 In him was life, and that life was the light of all mankind. 5 The light shines in the darkness, and the darkness has not overcome it. 14 The Word became flesh and made his dwelling among us. We have seen his glory, the glory of the one and only Son, who came from the Father, full of grace and truth."*
> (John 1:1-5, 14, NIV)

Adam is the beginning of humanity leading to death: Jesus is the new beginning leading to eternal life. Adam is the seed of humanity; Jesus is the new shoot of humanity and we in Christ are the harvest of humanity.

Time bows in recognition of the Eternal Son. He is the dawn of a new beginning and the Gospel of John begins as another genesis; time literally starts again in recognition of the entrance not just of another son but of the one and only Son. Jesus is not just another son He is the Eternal Son who became flesh and dwelt among us. There is no other, He is the one and only Son. John marks this new Genesis in his opening words. It is as significant a beginning as the first Genesis but even greater in that this beginning marks the entrance of the Son who would not fail and who would demonstrate the grace and love of God to fallen Adamic humanity. John pulls no punches: this Son is God Himself poured into humanity; He is the eternal Son; the eternal Word made flesh.

"For in Him all the fullness of Deity (the Godhead) dwells in bodily form [completely expressing the divine essence of God]." (Colossians 2:9, Amplified Bible)

Yet in his humanity, total humility is demonstrated, since like all other men He has to wait on time for the unveiling of His identity and purpose on earth. He is totally God and totally man, **Son of God, Son of man**. As Adam encapsulated all humanity on earth as the first man, so Jesus the Christ will encapsulate all the redeemed as the one and only righteous Son of God.

Romans 5:17 (NIV) states: *"For if, by the trespass of the one man, death reigned through that one man, how much more will those who receive God's abundant provision of grace and of the gift of righteousness reign in life through the one man, Jesus Christ!"*

I am making great emphasis on this point because it is imperative that we understand in this great revelation of our redemption to Sonship that Jesus does not just become another son, it is only in Him that we are sons. Time begins again with Christ, and even as Adam carried all humanity in his loins, so Jesus carries all believers in Himself as the Eternal Son. Jesus is not just a generic son in the sense that all humanity can claim to be children of God; He is the Divine Logos, the Word that has become flesh.

It is vital that we understand that Jesus the Christ, the Eternal Logos, has come from outside the limitations of time, thus dividing time and creating a new beginning. Even sinful men recognised this entry by changing the count of the international calendar to revolve around Christ. He the Eternal One is the only one qualified to be the source of this new beginning as He being God has no beginning and is able to be the source of pure life. This Genesis is not just a resetting of the world clock, it marks the beginning of the realignment of mankind in their purposed destiny as sons of God.

Neither Adam nor the sons of Adam could do this for their birthright was already forsaken in Eden. *"For all have sinned, and come short of the glory of God,"* (Romans 3:23, KJV) and all were corrupted and infected by the disease of sin and death. So there had to be another from heaven to create a new beginning with the integrity of the identity 'Son of God' intact and uncorrupted. Only such a one would be qualified to usher in once again divine creative order into the physical realm. Here spiritual connection with the physical realm, through the sons of God, would be rightly reinstalled. After the search of heaven and earth, only one could qualify, Jesus the Christ the Son of the living God.

"[1] Then I saw in the right hand of him who sat on the throne a scroll with writing on both sides and sealed with seven seals. [2] And I saw a mighty angel proclaiming in a loud voice, "Who is worthy to break the seals and open the scroll?" [3] But no one in heaven or on earth or under the earth could open the scroll or even look inside it. [4] I wept and wept because no one was found who was worthy to open the scroll or look inside. [5] Then one of the elders said to me, "Do not weep! See, the Lion of the tribe of Judah, the Root of David, has triumphed. He is able to open the scroll and its seven seals."

[6] Then I saw a Lamb, looking as if it had been slain, standing at the centre of the throne, encircled by the four living creatures and the elders. The Lamb had seven horns and seven eyes, which are the seven spirits of God sent out into all the earth. [7] He went and took the scroll from the right hand of him who sat on the throne. [8] And when he had taken it, the four living creatures and the twenty-four elders fell down before the Lamb. Each one had a harp and they were holding golden bowls full of incense, which are the prayers of God's people.

[9] And they sang a new song, saying:

"You are worthy to take the scroll and to open its seals, because you were slain, and with your blood you purchased for God persons from every tribe and language and people and nation. [10] You have made them to be a kingdom and

priests to serve our God, and they will reign on the earth." (Revelations 5:1-10, NIV)

Your REFLECTIONS

Make a list of why Jesus is qualified to be Saviour and Lord.

Chapter 11: Godhead Communications

> "...so that they may be one as we are one."
> (John 17:22, NIV)

The communication process within the Godhead is so perfect that it is rightly described as *one*. The mantra of the Jews is *"the Lord our God is one"*.

The communication process within the Godhead is always at its optimum frequency and it is beyond the limitations of time and space. It is innumerably faster than the speed of light and infinitely more precise in clarity than anything beneath the heavens. The communication process is beyond sight, touch, sound, smell, or taste, for it is by the Spirit. Not by might with the speed of transfer, or by power in terms of accuracy of the message, but by the Spirit of God. The communication process is from Spirit to Spirit by Spirit. The system has perfect integrity, and nothing is lost in transition.

The total message is sent, and the total message is received. There is no time lapse and there is no obstacle of distance as this communication process is operating outside the limitations of time and space. The Godhead are in one eternal atmosphere of Spirit where every movement is felt, every sound is heard, every fragrance is smelt, every vista is seen, and every taste is savoured.

Father, Son, and Holy Spirit are always in perfect synchronisation. When John caught a glimpse of this great glory, he magnificently concluded "*God is love*". As Christians we can rightly join with the Jewish mantra: "*The Lord our God is one*".

It is important however to say that because their seamless union is beyond the measurements of this world, this does not mean that we should migrate to the understanding that they are not distinct in persons. The persons within the Godhead are not a charade or a fabrication. Jesus is actually praying to the Father and not to Himself; the Holy Spirit is another, not the same Comforter.

The relationship within God is to be honoured and valued as a real presentation of perfected union. It can only be a real perfect union if there is a clear distinction in persons. This real relationship operating in the perfect incorruptible atmosphere of spirit and expressed with the purest love, is the relationship which is the pattern for all relationships. This relationship is eternal, it has always existed.... "*in the beginning God*". If this was not the pre-creation reality, then God could not be love as acknowledged by John.

The prerequisite of love is relationship, and it is out of this eternal relationship of love, this Godhead communication, that God who is Spirit embarked on creating the physical realm. I sometimes put it this way: what was going on in God was so gloriously fantastic that out of the overflow of His generosity, motivated by love, He chose to share this glory by creating a visible physical realm. This sharing was never going to be a simple process as it would involve the Creator making Himself vulnerable to the rebellion of His creation, as choice is a necessary component of love. It is an elaborate and ingenious plan.

God's plan to share could not fail as He knows the end from the beginning and therefore is so able to order the process that failure is impossible. It is often cited in our projection of biblical history that our infinite God was so shocked by the fall of man that He altered His plan from merely enjoying fellowship, to redeeming man. The more precise narrative is that God factored the fall into His unchanging eternal plan of extending His invisible Kingdom into visibility. Jesus was always central to that plan hence from the foundation of the world the Lamb was slain (I Peter 1:19-20, Revelation 13:8) and the plan was set in motion knowing that man would fall.

Man was made as a spiritual being with a physical body, a place of intersection between two realms, the spiritual and the physical. This design was key to God's plan to share Himself. Central to the plan is God sharing God and central to that is Godhead communication. God's plan is intricate and detailed, spanning from before time and space to beyond time and space. He purposed to extend the glory of His oneness to the confines of visibility. It is an elaborate and ingenious plan. He not only created image bearers; He created a story. He demonstrated His love in grace and mercy by redeeming the most undeserving to the position of 'sons'.

God's plan involves extending His most intimate perfect circle of oneness to include a sea of believers who are fitted together in Christ. We have been given access to the executive channel of communication; we have been accorded a seat within the executives of the Kingdom.

"And hath raised us up together, and made us sit together in heavenly places in Christ Jesus". (Ephesians 2:6, KJV)

We are allowed access beyond just having a conversation; we become partakers in divine privilege and are invited to bask in His oneness.

> "*21 That they all may be one; as thou, Father, art in me, and I in thee, that they also may be one in us: that the world may believe that thou hast sent me. 22 And the glory which thou gavest me I have given them; that they may be one, even as we are one: 23 I in them, and thou in me, that they may be made perfect in one; and that the world may know that thou hast sent me, and hast loved them, as thou hast loved me.*" (John 17:21-23, KJV)

Oneness is not just about us enjoying intimacy with one another; it is about each of us being partakers of the oneness that is in God. The ultimate intimacy is oneness. In God is the place of oneness: as we find oneness with God, we discover oneness with each other. True oneness is not located in a song or in the gift of music or in a well preached sermon or in the euphoria of a crowd; true oneness is located in our Triune God. As we discover oneness in Him we also discover oneness with others who are also located in Christ in God.

Enoch walked with God and he was no more, he got so deep in oneness that he simply could not return. (Genesis 5:24)

Moses was so exposed to the glory of oneness that he became a human light bulb. (Exodus 34:29-35)

Jesus was walking in oneness. "*In him dwells the fullness of the Godhead bodily.*" (Colossians 2:9, KJV). "*I and the*

Father are one." (John 10:30, NIV). *"Anyone who has seen me has seen the Father."* (John 14:9, NLT); *"I do whatever I see my Father doing"*. (John 5:19).

As we partake in the oneness of God, so we become one with our fellow partakers. Key to the plan of God then is the extension of Godhead communications to the visible physical realm through the sea of believers presenting themselves as living sacrifices (Romans 12:1).

> *"Through these he has given us his very great and precious promises, so that through them you may participate in the divine nature, having escaped the corruption in the world caused by evil desires."* (2 Peter 1:4, NIV)

The glorious miraculous truth is that God in Christ has extended His intimate communication system beyond the invisible spiritual realm, to a visible physical realm.

We can glimpse this communication process in the spiritual phenomena of prayer. We can connect with God instantaneously, from wherever we are located. True prayer in its essence is a tool that enables our participation in oneness.

"... that they may be one as we are one." (John 17:22, NIV)

It is important however, that we do not minimise the significance of this privilege although it can be accessed through prayer. It is much more than the tool for prayer. God has given us in Christ access to His internal Godhead communication system. We have been given access to that which makes God One. This is a crazy ridiculous honour. However, it is real and that is what Peter infers to when he speaks of participating in the divine nature.

Even the spotless heavenly beings do not get access to the internal Godhead communication system; however, we the redeemed believers in Christ have been invited to participate in His Oneness. The Holy Spirit has elevated us in Christ into the very inner circle of God. We are seated in heavenly places in Christ Jesus. Of course, if we were uncovered, we would die from being exposed to such a holy atmosphere, but in the covering of Christ we truly live.

This is the abundant life promised to all believers in the centre of the exalted Christ. We often reduce the concept of abundance to the wealth of the earth and the best physical and psychological sensations; abundance is so much more than that. Abundant life is to be spiritually positioned in the centre of the exalted Christ. It is to be centred in the very source of life itself. We are predestined to experience life in its purest form, surging through our being. We are placed in the centre of Christ by the Holy Spirit as He sits in the deep spirit of His Father. This is the source environment of spirit, the Holy of Holies, and in this oneness we experience Godhead communications.

Your REFLECTIONS

Write to God. Let Him know what you think of Him giving you access to His personal communication system.

Chapter 12: Son of God Versus Children of God - No opt out

> *"But as many as received him, to them gave He power to become the sons of God, even to them that believe on his name: Which were born, not of blood, nor of the will of the flesh, nor of the will of man, but of God."* (John 1:12-13, KJV)

For many years I have heard believers use such language as 'I am trying to live the Christian life', as if you can be a partial Christian in your identity. Others make the supposedly humble claim to being a sinner saved by grace. If we are still identifying as sinners, then what exactly has grace achieved? I am not suggesting that we do not sin, but if we, as recipients of salvation, are at our core still sinners, then are we not diminishing God's act of grace to us? As we have been exposed to the revelation of Sonship, some believers have more readily accepted the identity of 'children of God', yet have shown some reluctance in accepting the identity 'son of God', as if it is too large a claim to embrace. Yes, it is a large claim but there is no opting out of the identity of Sonship in salvation. We are saved to Sonship with all its glorious implications.

We cannot easily deny our identity as a son of man, as daily we are faced with the reality of our evident humanity, but this is generally a far cry from the immutable perfection of Deity. Therefore, 'son of man' in the fallen state we accept, but 'son of God'? How could that be?

Such thinking is too lofty, it is ridiculous. Yes, we are members of the human race, and some of us even struggle with that and reduce humans to just another animal. Many will go as far as accepting that we are members of the generic 'children of God' as created beings, but to claim to be a 'son of God' would be a step too far. then, we can end up accepting a status based on our judgement and yet end up rejecting the Word of God.

In the parable of the lost son, as he returned, the son said to the father "make me like one of your hired servants". We might think that this is a statement of humility, but it is in fact sin. Just because one bows his or her knees does not mean they are not full of pride. In fact, Jesus alluded to this in His teaching on prayer. He said not everyone who addresses God as Lord shall enter the Kingdom. Although the prodigal son was heading in the right direction, he still needed to be transformed. It is as if he was saying, *"I am coming, but I need to make myself right."* Or *"I will come Lord, but on my terms."* If you throw yourself on the mercy of God, you do not have any say about your position; it is His decision.

Often the way we come can be our ultimate stumbling block, we want Him as Saviour but not as Lord. It looked like humility when the lost son returned with his line *"make me like your hired servants"*, but the greater humility is *"Whatever you say, Lord."* The greater response of humility is *"Yes, Lord"*. The Sonship revelation is not about us being a mere member of the

Creator's global family of creation, rather it is about us being the very Son of the Creator.

We cannot come to Him and then reject His purpose; we cannot come and contradict His plan. Yet we struggle with the extent of God's generosity and in some cases insist on settling for a lesser status than 'Son'. The plan and purpose of God is not reactionary, it is essentially set in Himself before the beginning. In Hebrews Chapter One, God reveals His plan to reveal Himself through His Son. Jesus is that Son, the only begotten Son, the spirit container of all believers past present and future. Sonship is not an option-it is the only option for the believer.

"For there is no other name under heaven by which we must be saved." (Acts 4:12, NLT)

Are you insisting on staying in the shadows? Are you insisting on being anonymous, staying in the background? Are you saying *yes* to salvation but *no* to His Lordship? I put it to you that this is not the act of humility but rather the sin of pride. It is like being a special guest at a dinner party: you arrive at the house, but then refuse to go beyond the entrance, thus rejecting your position at the table. How would you feel if you were the host? How insulted would you be after making eternal preparation for your guest?

This is not some new teaching. This is the eternal plan of God that we might be fitted together in Christ, occupying the position of *son*. Why Son? - because He is Son and we are in Christ. It must be Son and can only be Son. It does not matter if you are male or female, Jew or Gentile, the position for all who would be saved has to be in Christ the Son. He is the Spirit-carrier, the Ark of the redeemed.

Hence, we are appropriately described as the Body of Christ. *"What about my femininity or masculinity or my blackness or my whiteness or my Jewish or Gentile heritage?"*

The answer remains the same - the only position available in the Kingdom to believers (it is also the highest position), is 'son'. Our individual identities are not negated but rather they are founded in the identity of Christ. Therefore, if you are female, that characteristic becomes perfected in Christ; if you are black or white that characteristic also becomes perfected; if you are Jew or Gentile those characteristics become perfected in Christ, they are not negated. We enter individually and then as a community of believers we are fitted together, collectively becoming the one Body of Christ. The chosen Son as is foreshadowed by Joseph in the Old Testament, is clothed with a coat of many colours, representing His diverse makeup.

The claim to be a son of God is as bold as the grace released to bring us into that Sonship from the vilest sin; that is the demonstration of the generous and powerful nature of God's grace. This, my dearly beloved, is core to the display of an invisible God in a visible world. God's visible demonstration of Himself is through His wonderful and marvellous creation of us in His image as spirit beings. It is through His incarnation, obedient life, death and resurrection, and also through the deliverance of mankind from the vilest of sins. Also central to His visible manifestation is the change of our status as born-again believers from orphans to sons of God. You are more than an animal; you are not just a member of the generic 'children of God': you are a 'son of God'.

Your REFLECTIONS

Note examples where your 'humility' might actually have been pride in disguise.

Note examples when instead of doing what you wanted, you said yes and did what God wanted. How did your obedience impact your life?

Chapter 13: The Corporate Son of God

> "*15 Instead, speaking the truth in love, we will grow to become in every respect the mature body of him who is the head, that is, Christ. 16 From him the whole body, joined and held together by every supporting ligament, grows and builds itself up in love, as each part does its work.*" (Ephesians 4:15, 16, NIV)

"By one spirit are we baptised into one body." (1 Corinthians 12:13, NIV)

Living in a fallen world and accepting the frailty of humanity is not a problem for most of us, but to accept the perfection of Deity is often seen as reaching beyond our station. Words such as 'pride' and 'blasphemy' come to mind. **Son of man, Son of God** can become a challenging conundrum. How can this be? Of course, the claim to being a son of God could certainly cross the line into blasphemy, as it has done historically with men who have claimed such a position independently of Christ.

Let us consider: if we can claim to be 'son of man' because of the one man Adam, why can we not claim to be Son of God because of the one Son of God, Christ? Maybe that is not such a stretch after all. If we can be linked spiritually and physically to our ancestor Adam, why can we not also be linked spiritually and physically to the Eternal Son who became flesh and made His dwelling among us? You see our relationship to Adam is a type or shadow of the eternally purposed relationship with Jesus the Christ. As the many have descended from the one Adam, how much more shall the many ascend through the one Eternal Son?

> "*45 So it is written: "The first man Adam became a living being, the last Adam, a life-giving spirit. 46 The spiritual did not come first, but the natural, and after that the spiritual. 47 The first man was of the dust of the earth; the second man is of heaven. 48 As was the earthly man, so are those who are of the earth; and as is the heavenly man, so also are those who are of heaven. 49 And just as we have borne the image of the earthly man, so shall we bear the image of the heavenly man.*" (1 Corinthians 15:45-49, NIV)

The physical realm was always intended to be a visible display of the invisible spiritual realm. From this we see God's intention in the process of time and space, which is to perfect His unchanging eternal plan. We do not generally deny our being one human race based on differences in gender, culture, or ethnic groups. We are all 'sons of man'. Likewise, as believers we can see this as being a type of our spiritual link to Christ where gender, culture and ethnicity do not negate our membership of the body of Christ.

The claim to be a son of God is based totally on our individual relationship with Christ. There is no Son of God outside of Jesus the Christ. In John Chapter Fifteen, Jesus describes Himself as the true vine. It is clear, that one must be a part of the vine. The vine is a fantastic illustration of the intimate and intricate relationship that is a prerequisite to Sonship. You simply cannot claim Sonship outside of Christ. In Christ, branches that are not in the vine are only fit for firewood. Jesus said in John 15:6, NIV:

> "6 If you do not remain in me, you are like a branch that is thrown away and withers; such branches are picked up, thrown into the fire and burned."

This is a strong statement and 'son' is a relational term. It is a harsh but fair reminder that there is no Sonship outside of relationship. Any teaching that promotes the belief of a position of 'son of God' that is independent of Christ has crossed the line into blasphemy. You cannot say you are a son of God and not be in relationship with Jesus. The two are inextricably linked.

As much as I am a strong advocate for the security of salvation, a person who is obviously not in relation with the Lord Jesus even though they claim some historical experience, is in contradiction of the Word. Jesus said, *"You shall know them by their fruit."* (Matthew 7:15, NIV) There is simply no salvation outside of Sonship and there is no Sonship outside of relationship with Jesus. Maybe those who make such a claim are the branches that have been fruitless in verse two of John Chapter Fifteen that the Father has cut off, or they may be like the seed in the parable of the sower that never found good soil. The simple fact is there is no Sonship outside of an in-Christ relationship. I do not believe it is a different rule for the Catholic, Anglican, Baptist, Methodist, Pentecostals,

Charismatics or Independents; in every case there must be a living relationship with Jesus through the Holy Spirit.

A claim to be a son without a living relationship with the Son and based purely on some historical event, experience or ceremony is a biblically flawed posture. Some would make a claim solely on being baptised as a baby, or solely on passing through a confirmation ceremony or on being baptised as an adult, or on regularity of attendance at a particular church, or on theological qualifications or based on past or present leadership roles in church organisations, or even on a past response for salvation by making a prayer of repentance.

All these factors might hold some value, however the most critical to the claim to Sonship is: *"Are you in a living relationship with Jesus the Christ as your Lord and Saviour?"* I am positively not advocating legalism in the sense that we have to work to be saved; but I am declaring with clarity that there is definitively no Sonship or salvation outside of the grace that is in Christ. The Father Himself declared that Jesus the Christ is His Son in whom He is well pleased.

Our Sonship identity is bound to His identity as defined by the Father.

The next salient point in terms of making biblical sense of our call to Sonship and why it does not negate our femininity or our ethnicity or our being Gentiles, is the understanding that we are not being called to be male or Jewish. Rather we are being called to be fitted together as the corporate body of Christ the Son of God, so *Son of God* is plurality in one. That itself sounds like the reflection of God. The son is the perfect physical extension of the reach of an invisible God into a visible physical realm. This revelation of the son being plurality in oneness gives greater resonance to the prayer "*so that they may be one as we are one.*" (John 17:22, NIV) The Kingdom of God is rightly extended through the presence of the King; there is no more perfect King than the Eternal Son.

I have sometimes struggled with calling women, 'sons of God' as such a term does not fit with feminine identity. However, in understanding that the Son of God is corporate, we now understand that whether male or female, Jew or Gentile, black or white we all as believers are assembled together as the body of the corporate son of God.

> "*[15] Instead, speaking the truth in love, we will grow to become in every respect the mature body of him who is the head, that is, Christ. [16] From him the whole body, joined and held together by every supporting ligament, grows and builds itself up in love, as each part does its work.*" (Ephesians 4:15, 16, NIV)

We are collectively in Christ the Son of God. Jesus the Christ is the Spirit-carrier, the ark for all believers. Even as Adam was sufficient to lead all humanity from God into unrighteousness, so Jesus is more than sufficient to carry us in righteousness back to God. Within that collective as members of the body of the Son, we can individually claim to be sons of God. Even as members of one human race we can claim individually to be human. Jesus said, when you pray individually you can address God as

'Father'. The Son of God became the Son of Man, that the sons of men might become the corporate Son of God.

The third salient point is that our Sonship is qualified by our being led by the Spirit of God. *"For as many as are led by the Spirit of God, they are the sons of God."* (Romans 8:14, KJV)

Any sense of our being puffed up with pride with the blessing of Sonship can only be described as seriously ridiculous in the light of these fundamental checks and balances.

Sonship requires the son to be clearly navigated by the Holy Spirit. There is no Sonship without this qualification. Even as Christ was specifically led by the Holy Spirit, we also must know His leading individually and collectively. Our intimate relationship with the Holy Spirit is key to our identity as sons. He places us in the body of Christ, and He indwells our body. *"For by one Spirit are we all baptised into one body."* (1 Corinthians 12:13a, KJV)

We need to be indwelt, filled, baptised, led, and sealed by the Holy Spirit. The role of the Holy Spirit is intrinsic to Sonship. He is not a marginalised, effervescent, optional experience of Pentecostals or Charismatics, He is central to the eternal purpose of God as the One who implements the extension of the invisible God into a visible world through the Son. Sonship is a call to intimacy; this intimacy can only be enacted through the works of the Holy Spirit.

To summarise:

- There is no Sonship outside of a living relationship with Christ.

- Being a son does not negate our gender or culture, rather our unique characteristics are perfected as we are incorporated into the Kingdom culture of the Son.
- Sonship demands the prerequisite of being led by the Holy Spirit.

Your REFLECTIONS

What does it mean to have a living relationship with Jesus?

Chapter 14: He Does the Glory

> *"He will glorify me because it is from me that he will receive what he will make known to you."*
> (John 16:14, NIV)

When we go to an ice-cream parlour, besides having numerous choices of ice-cream we also have numerous choices of toppings which are often described as optional extras. These can increase the wonder of the dining experience, but they are not essential. Unfortunately, church history has misinformed us of the role of the Holy Spirit, making Him an optional extra. Besides the works of the Holy Spirit being marginalised to Pentecostals and Charismatics, we also see Him being promoted among Pentecostals and Charismatics as an extra topping.

This is not intended to condemn the Pentecostal or Charismatic movements because they brought an essential platform to a Christianity that had largely relegated the living works of the Holy Spirit to history. It is to help us understand that new movements introduce new thinking which can be so polarised around a particular experience that the essential message of divine purpose can become obscured. We could easily do this again by not linking the revelation of Sonship with the living works of the Holy Spirit.

Jesus said, *"He shall glorify me"* (John 16:14, KJV). The works of the Holy Spirit were always more than just the event of baptism with the spirit or the event of a miracle.

His purpose must and always be one with the eternal purpose of God, decided and sealed in God before creation began. The Holy Spirit, in humility as an invisible member of the Godhead, is the One at work among humanity to implement the extension of the invisible God into the visible realm.

He makes us one with the Eternal Son. He is the One that places us in Christ, so we then become partakers of His Sonship. Since the Holy Spirit fits us together as one within the body of Christ, He is responsible for plurality in oneness. The Holy Spirit then transcends time and space, intricately connecting the corporate body of the Son to the invisible executive Godhead of the heavenly realm, causing a passage of glory to flow between the invisible and the visible. This flow of glory is the stream that makes glad the city of God. How can this be? He does the glory.

For the Holy Spirit to achieve the purposes of God He does micro work in us and then He does macro work with us. He does the glory. We however can become so overwhelmed and fixated on His work within us that we end up frustrating His work with us. Due to the wonder of His work within, we can easily fail to understand that the detailed micro work within us is a prerequisite of His glorious macro work with us.

The Holy Spirit positions Christ in us through His indwelling presence, placing us within the body of Christ. 'Salvation' and 'Sonship' are part of the same work of grace. Just knowing that the Holy Spirit has done this is reason enough to have an eternal praise party. Hence, we can get so excited with this amazing act; in so doing we might end up refusing to embrace any further work of grace.

Jesus baptises us with the Holy Spirit, enabling us to be supernaturally empowered for Sonship. We are encouraged to be filled with the Holy Spirit so that we can display the fruit of the Spirit, which is the character of the Son. How many have become so enthralled with power that we have lost sight of purpose? Or how many, because of the precise work of the Holy Spirit on our characters, have begun to see ourselves as the end purpose, causing us to miss His eternal purpose?

The Holy Spirit replaces our soulish navigation system by rectifying our internal sinful disorder with a Spirit-led navigation system, so we are rewired with the navigation of Sonship. *For those that are led by the Spirit are the Sons of God.* Instead of relying on our rational and sensory tools for leadership, which make up instruments of our soul, we are navigated by our spirit which is in communion with the Holy Spirit. The rational and sensory tools of the soul are then well placed to support the leadership of the Spirit. There is no Sonship without the Holy Spirit, as Jesus said He does the glory. This is not founded in intellect or acute use of sensory ability; Sonship is founded in the work of the Holy Spirit. "*Not by might nor by power but by My Spirit*"; (Zechariah 4:6, NKJV) He does the glory.

The Holy Spirit performs the work of sealing (2 Corinthians 1:22, Ephesians 1:13, Ephesians 4:30) where He literally crowns us with royalty. The essence of the word 'sealing' in this instance is to sanction a transaction or an agreement. The Holy Spirit gives us the ring and robe of son and He gives us the crown of royalty. How can this be? Sonship is the intricately miraculous work of grace by the Holy Spirit. He does the glory. With this amazing work of grace within us by the Holy Spirit, it can easily be understood how one can start assuming that this must be the end purpose of God. Although this internal work of grace is amazing, it is but the prerequisite to the further work of grace with us. The Holy Spirit does the work within us to create Sonship so He can do the work with us as sons.

"For we are God's handiwork, created in Christ Jesus to do good works, which God prepared in advance for us to do." (Ephesians 2:10, NIV)

Assembled together, we are the body of the eternal Son representing the invisible Father in the visible physical realm. Hallelujah! He does the glory. There is no Sonship without the glory and there is no glory without the Holy Spirit. He does the glory. The gall of seeing the works of the Holy Spirit as optional to Sonship is the pinnacle of religious arrogance and an exhibit of total absurdity. He does the glory. Without the Holy Spirit we make religion, we develop rituals, our Christianity becomes an institution not a living body, it becomes a corpse without breath. Jesus said it, we need to get it. *He does the glory.*

It is important to reiterate that the work of the Holy Spirit within us to create Sonship is but a prerequisite for His further work with us as sons; this will be the focus of the successive chapters.

Your REFLECTIONS

What place does the Holy Spirit have in your everyday life?

Chapter 15: The Age of the Son

"In the past God spoke to our ancestors through the prophets at many times and in various ways, but in these last days he has spoken to us by his Son, whom he appointed heir of all things, and through whom also he made the universe." (Hebrews 1:1, NIV).

We are living in the most significant time ever; we are living in the age of the Son. To be around with the renowned prophets such as Elijah and Elisha must have been great, but nothing can top the age of the Son. The creation groans in anticipation for the revealing of the sons of God. Isaiah, in the year that King Uzziah died, had a vision of this Son high and lifted up and His train filling the temple (Isaiah 6 v 1). We are that train, the very body of Christ extended into the earth. We are not just sons by assumption; we are sons by the glorious, detailed work of the Holy Spirit, on display for all to see like the train of a bride's dress. We are the transforming entourage of the eternal King. We are that visible impacting army that is too innumerable to count.

We are the sons of God that the earth was craving for and anticipating since it was created, even before it was scorched by the impact of Adam's sin. In Christ Jesus we spiritually possess the answer to the earth's most ailing need. We are sons of God and we together are 'Son of God', plurality in oneness. It is the age of the Son, a glorious age when the invisible God has made Himself visible in the physical reality of the corporate Son.

We are sons by blood, by birth, and by spirit and to refute any challenge, we are sons by legal adoption.

1. We are sons by *blood* in that Jesus was divinely conceived in a virgin by the Holy Spirit and this blood was poured out for us that we might receive His life, the life of the Son.

2. We are sons by *birth*. Jesus said, "*Verily, verily, you must be born again.*" (John 3:3) It is through new birth that we enter the family of God.

3. We are sons by *spirit*.

   "*[14] For those who are led by the Spirit of God are the children of God. [15] The Spirit you received does not make you slaves, so that you live in fear again; rather, the Spirit you received brought about your adoption to sonship. And by him we cry, "Abba, Father." [16] The Spirit Himself testifies with our spirit that we are God's children.*" (Romans 8:14-16, KJV)

4. We are sons by *adoption*.

   "*[4] But when the set time had fully come, God sent his Son, born of a woman, born under the law, [5] to redeem those under the law, that we might receive adoption to sonship. [6] Because you are his sons, God sent the Spirit of his Son into our hearts, the Spirit who calls out, "Abba, Father." [7] So you are no longer a slave, but God's child; and since you are his child, God has made you also an heir.*" (Galatians 4:4-7, NIV)

We are the ultimate representation of the Father, even as listed in the parable of the Tenants (Luke 20 v9-19). When the master sent his son there was no greater representative. He was the heir of the father and therefore the wicked tenants understood that he had the right of ownership. The age of the son is the age of exact representation and it is the age of ownership. The son is the rightful heir of the father.

The ministry of prophet, priest and king are all great, however they are but forerunners to the entrance of the Son who encapsulates these ministries and goes further in sharing the very nature of His Father as God. To the prophets, the priest and the king, God is their master but to the Son, He is Father. The prophets, the priests and kings are workers within the Kingdom of God, the Son is God in flesh, Emmanuel. The prophets, the priests and kings are messengers of God, while the Son is the Message.

> "*1 In the beginning was the Word, and the Word was with God, and the Word was God. 2 He was with God in the beginning. 3 Through him all things were made; without him nothing was made that has been made. 4 In him was life, and that life was the light of all mankind. ... 14 The Word became flesh and made his dwelling among us. We have seen his glory, the glory of the one and only Son, who came from the Father, full of grace and truth.*" (John 1:1-4, 14, NIV).

In times past God spoke through types and symbols. He spoke through fallible prophets, priests, and even kings;

now in the fullness of time He speaks more directly and precisely through His manifested Son. This is the age of the Son. The owner and the Creator of all things has stepped physically into His creation. He is the Eternal Son and the earth tremors with each of His steps as its core recognises the weight of His presence.

Every type, each symbolism and every messianic prophecy all find their culmination in the age of the Son. God has no greater clarity in communication than Son. He is the Word made flesh. The age of the Son cannot be superseded, there is no greater prophet, there is no further Messiah, there is no additional son or daughter of God. Jesus the Christ is God's best and most perfect representative. We are called to be conformed to His image for there is no greater image of God than Jesus the Christ who is the Son of the living God. In Him there is perfect integrity and clarity of communication. All valid prophecy is given to support and validate God's speech through *Son*. We the church are the body of Christ fitted together in the oneness of the Spirit to amplify the sound of the Son.

Your REFLECTIONS

Why is it great to be living in the Age of the Son?

Chapter 16: A Matter of Identity

> "*4 Jesus, knowing all that was going to happen to him, went out and asked them, "Who is it you want?" 5 "Jesus of Nazareth," they replied. "I am he," Jesus said. (And Judas the traitor was standing there with them.). 6 When Jesus said, "I am he," they drew back and fell to the ground."* (John 18:4-6, NIV)

The earth is created by God to recognise who we are. The physical realm is dependent on the spiritual realm for its life source. The earth is pre-programmed to naturally respond to the majestic authority of the Eternal Son. This is not just a question of power but of authority which is founded in identity. Jesus undoubtedly had power which was balanced with His authority. When there is power without the balance of authority then power has to flaunt itself for effect, but when there is a residing authority, your very presence exudes power. Power is rooted in authority which is rooted in identity.

Before Jesus spoke, before He healed one sick person, before He drove out one demon, He had authority. Jesus had authority in His identity as the Eternal Son. Just as a plant is predisposed to bend towards the light, so the earth reacts to the presence of the Lord. The earth is hard wired to respond to the presence of the sons of God.

> "*19 For the earnest expectation of the creature waiteth for the manifestation of the sons of God.*

> [22] *For we know that the whole creation groaneth and travaileth in pain together until now.* (Romans 8:19, 22, KJV)

It is important to note that even before we do anything as members of the body of Christ, the earth is already responding to who we are. The grace of Sonship causes the earth to bend towards us in a posture of worship even when we are yet to fully understand the authority and the power that we carry.

As a new baby, Jesus had no cognitive idea of who He was, yet He was being worshipped by the wise men and the shepherds; all He had to do was show up: His very presence caused the Earth to bow. Hallelujah! All you have to do is show up and your identity as 'son' will evoke a response. Just as His identity carried authority, your identity as 'son' also carries authority.

Then Jesus came to them and said, *"All authority in heaven and on earth has been given to me."* (Matthew 28: 18, KJV)

Too many people are wandering around trying to operate in power, not understanding that it is in authority that true power resides. Power was in His identity as a Son; power is in authority and authority is in identity. As plants must bend towards light so the Earth must bow in the presence of the Son of the living God. It is a matter of identity and it obeys the principles of true science. True science is not just based on the partial understanding that we have discovered through time but rather on the total knowledge of God. We need to understand that the physical realm is predisposed to react to the very identity of the sons of God.

Do not be amazed when your shadow causes healing and deliverance. Just showing up in obedience to the Holy Spirit will bring deliverance. The earth bows in anticipation as it sees the approach of the son just waiting for the command of your voice. Do not underestimate the stir which your presence creates, it is a matter of identity. Jesus was challenged several times with the question "*if you are the son of God*". Since there was full integrity in His identity, as Son, He did not need to respond to the innate seed of doubt that was in this challenge, He instead chose to focus on following the leading of the Holy Spirit.

When you know your identity as a son of God, you do not need to prove it, rather focus on following the leading of the Holy Spirit. It is a matter of identity; just show up and whatsoever the Holy Spirit says, do it. The world will challenge us, it will ask the question about our credentials. Darkness and the prince of the power of the air will be offended by us and will seek to crush and discredit us. However, our focus should not be to reach for our spiritual CV or identity cards, but rather on submitting to the navigation of the Holy Spirit. Our concern should be hearing and responding to the voice of the Holy Spirit; we must therefore diligently resist the seeds of deception of the accuser.

It is no surprise that at the beginning of Jesus's ministry He was bombarded by questions of His identity. Jesus in the crux of physical vulnerability was bombarded with questions demanding proof of Sonship. But Jesus did not have to prove what was not in doubt and He certainly did not have to waste time proving His identity to Satan.

It can be incredibly life-impacting not knowing your birth parents; people have been known to spend a lifetime searching for their birth family in the hope that the inner questions of origin and identity will be answered. Father God does not want us confused and in doubt about our relationship with Him. He wants us so sure that the slightest doubt is not entertained. He wants us so secure that even in a hostile world our focus is 'what next', and 'where next, Holy Spirit'?

My 23 year old son looks like me (although he would claim to be more handsome), he has my temperament (although he claims to be more humorous), and he was raised by me with some help from my wife (dad humour). With all these facts, he does not question his physical identity or origin, he can simply engage with the process of living. Likewise, God the Father wants us to be so secure in our identity as His sons that we can literally get on with following the leading of the Holy Spirit. God Himself has defined our Sonship, there is certainly no need to waste time proving this to Satan or any other. Our duty is to simply obey the voice of the Holy Spirit.

Paul in his letter to the Galatians keeps this quite succinct: *"Since we live by the Spirit, let us keep in step with the Spirit."* (Galatians 5:25, NIV)

It is a matter of identity: our authority resides in the integrity of who we are in Christ, as He is Son, so we are sons. With identity is authority and in authority resides true power to fulfil the purpose of the Father.

Your REFLECTIONS

How do others describe you?

How does God describe you?

Chapter 17: The Spirit of antiChrist: A Hostile Environment

"For our struggle is not against flesh and blood, but against the rulers, against the authorities, against the powers of this dark world and against the spiritual forces of evil in the heavenly realms." (Ephesians 6:12, NIV)

"In this world you will have trouble. But take heart! I have overcome the world." (John 16:33b, NIV)

Keeping in step with the Holy Spirit seems a straightforward instruction for the follower of Christ; the challenge is doing that within a hostile environment. One of the great stumbling blocks and cry of humanity is why does a loving God allow suffering? Why does He allow bad things to happen to good people? This is such a vex point that many as a result become the judge and jury of God, and often refuse to serve God.

Such suffering as when children die of horrible diseases, when men mutilate one another, when the lust for money or power causes the enslavement of generations of a whole ethnic group. "Lord God, why did You let my child die? Why did You let my father die? Why did You let my mother die?" "You cannot be a Good God, You must be evil, Amen."

There concludes the judgment of God by many, even though they have heard the argument that man has been given free choice and that the devil is the source of evil. They rightly conclude that God is all-powerful and therefore nothing happens without His permission and then they wrongly conclude that He must be evil. In this way they fatalistically, with their judgement, curse God and die.

It must be understood that the works of the devil are not about achieving insignificant wins amongst humanity, his desire is to overthrow God by thwarting His eternal plan. This is not a war over time-limited consequences, this is a war over eternity where the time-limiting factors become collateral damage to our enemy. The aim of the works of the devil by his acts of evil is not merely to end life or inflict pain but rather to poison the relationship of generations of men with their Creator God. We are not the centre of the war, rather we have a central role. The war is between our Spirit God Creator and the evil venomous forces of the devil and we as central characters to the eternal plan of God are caught up in the middle. We are living in a hostile environment.

God has only had and only needs one plan, God who is love, in the beginning motivated by love initiated His ingenious plan to share His invisible Spirit self in a visible physical realm. He did not need to do this. He was all sufficient in Himself, His very good loving nature propelled Him to share by creating.

"In the beginning God created..." (Gen 1: 1, KJV)

God created the physical realm for Christ, as it would be through Christ, His Son, that He would put His invisible self on visible display. Christ is represented as the tree of life in the Garden of Eden. He is the source of the physical realm's existence; the world was created by Him and for Him. John literally re-opens Genesis as He explains this in his gospel:

> "*1 In the beginning was the Word, and the Word was with God, and the Word was God. 2 He was with God in the beginning. 3 Through him all things were made; without him nothing was made that has been made. 4 In him was life, and that life was the light of all mankind.*" (John 1:1-4, NIV)

John goes on to clarify that the Word is God's Eternal Son, just in case we missed it.

> "*The Word became flesh and made his dwelling among us. We have seen his glory, the glory of the one and only Son, who came from the Father, full of grace and truth.*" (John 1:14, NIV)

The physical realm is made by the Son and needs the Son for its existence. In reality then, the physical realm cannot continue without Christ.

Conversely, it should also be noted that sin created a world system that relies on the absence of Christ. Christ to this world system is as kryptonite is to the fictitious marvel superman character. This world as created by sin has no choice but to be extremely hostile to Christ because it depends on the absence of Christ for its existence. Hence the term antiChrist is the spirit of this sinful world which is violently opposed to the presence of Christ. The mantra of this spirit is "the Son must be killed, eliminated and assassinated"; this is a mantra motivated by pure hatred. A murderous spirit was dispatched in pursuit of Jesus from His birth, and many Jewish babies were indiscriminately killed (Matthew 2:16-18). Joseph and Mary had to seek refuge in Egypt to protect the Son (Matthew 2:13-15). This spirit of antiChrist continued its pursuit climaxing in the crucifixion which was foiled by the resurrection. Hallelujah!

"The thief comes only to steal and kill and destroy". (John 10:10, NIV)

The charge of this spirit of the antiChrist is extreme violence against the Son of God as it depends on His absence for existence. Ironically the physical realm needs the Son of God to exist (Colossians 1: 16-17). This violent murderous hostility continues even more venomously in the age of the Son as time hurtles towards its end in eternity. However, often our battle is at the stage of the assassin in pursuit of the baby son who has no cognitive awareness of his identity or at the stage of the tempter sowing seeds of doubt regarding our identity in the wilderness (as when Jesus endured His notorious temptations at the beginning of His ministry.

Sometimes the most expedient response to hostility is to run: Joseph ran when pursued by Potiphar's wife, Mary and Joseph ran with baby Jesus when pursued by Herod. Sometimes running is the Holy Spirit led option. Yet we must also note that Joseph who is a type of Christ in the Old Testament did not remain a rejected insecure youth. As Joseph grew and discovered purpose, he learnt to face hostility in a foreign land and also from his own family.

Jesus did not remain a baby. As He grew in grace and truth He faced family, neighbours, sickness, demons, leaders, politicians until He faced the ultimate hostility: public execution on a cross bearing the sins of all humanity. Jesus did not remain a baby being pursued by assassins; He became the pursuer.

"The reason the Son of God appeared was to destroy the devil's work." (1 John 3:8, NIV)

Where God wants us to be is at the stage of maturity where we, knowing who we are, set our faces like a flint and head towards hostility; where we like Jesus, knowing who we are will take the posture of a servant. He wants us to be at the stage where we are so secure in Him that like Jesus, we offer our lives as living sacrifices. God wants us to be at the stage where we understand this sinful world is going to be naturally hostile to us as His sons, but in Sonship we hold the very purpose for the existence of the physical realm.

We as sons need to head to our 'Jerusalem'. Jerusalem represents the centre of the battle; it represents the capital, the heart, the brain, the place from which life flows, the place where the war is won or lost. Knowing who we are as sons, we are called to face hostility and head to Jerusalem the centre of the battle just like Jesus, as the Holy Spirit leads. It is imperative to emphasise however that we encounter hostility not only in Jerusalem but also on the perilous journey there.

The antiChrist spirit will seek to assassinate the Son wherever He may be found and there is no concern for collateral damage. This spirit operates within the fundamental principle of terror; it is the ultimate terrorist. It will single-mindedly out of pure hatred hunt to kill you as a baby, as a toddler, as an adolescent, as a young adult and as a mature son. It is important to understand that as identified sons of God we are in a combat zone. We are at war with an enemy whose very existence depends on ending us by any means necessary.

This war is not sanitised, there is no gentleman's rule book or code. The devil will use the most devious, filthy and ugly method and means to take us down. He will infiltrate our families and friends. He will infect, he will poison, he will lie, he will cheat, he will rape, he will abuse; there is no limit to the darkness which he will unleash to achieve his ends.

Sons of God, we are in a real war. As much as creation has breath-taking beauty, we are in a hostile environment.

Your REFLECTIONS

In this hostile environment, what is your stage of maturity as a son?

How do you advance to the stage of the one pursuing rather than just being pursued by enemy forces?

Chapter 18: Fully Resourced

> *"...he will crush your head, and you will strike his heel."* (Genesis 3:15, NIV)

As a 'son' we are not only fully equipped but we have access to the Father who has unlimited resources. We are equipped with the full armour of the Lord and we are resourced body, soul and spirit with every earthly or heavenly resource necessary for victory.

We are blessed with every spiritual blessing in Christ Jesus. Every gift that is necessary for our victory is made available to us and we are made available as gifts to other sons to ensure victory. Another word that encapsulates God's total provision for His sons is 'grace'. Grace is not just linked to many people's limited view of salvation; it is about God's extravagant outpouring of His wealth on us as His sons. Grace is a description of the totality of God's provision.

As a son you are not just supported by God in terms of provision, neither are you just a steward of God's provision, rather we are in the status of owners of grace. We are heirs of the Father and joint heirs with Jesus. As sons we are visible representatives of the Father as esteemed members of His Kingdom. To delve further, we are owners of His provision. As sons we have a stake of ownership in our father's estate. This is what the elder son missed in the parable of the lost son. The father said, "What is one fatted calf, it all belongs to you". As a son we are not hirelings, we are members of the royal family that own the Kingdom.

Therefore, by God's grace we are fully equipped and resourced for our purpose. We have the spiritual covering of sons, we look like sons as image bearers and we are involved in the activity of sons, destroying or dismantling the works of the devil. The Lord is your shepherd, you shall not lack. The righteous shall not be forsaken nor shall their seed be beggars. The Lord lavishes us with His grace and this grace is His strength being made perfect in our weakness.

The Bible also informs us that God provides us with a full armour in Christ; we are fully equipped. No expense is spared to ensure that we are fully resourced by the most innovative and effective armoury as sons of God. We must however obey the commands if we are to make use of these resources.

> *"13 Therefore put on the full armour of God, so that when the day of evil comes, you may be able to stand your ground, and after you have done everything, to stand. 14 Stand firm then, with the belt of truth buckled around your waist, with the breastplate of righteousness in place, 15 and with your feet fitted with the readiness that comes from the gospel of peace. 16 In addition to all this, take up the shield of faith, with which you can extinguish all the flaming arrows of the evil one. 17 Take the helmet of salvation and the sword of the Spirit, which is the word of God. (Ephesians 6:13- 17, NIV)*

The armour we are commanded to put on covers our body, soul, and spirit. It is multi-dimensional:

a) *Physically* we are safeguarded from attacks. It does not stop the attacks, but it can literally mitigate the effects.

b) *Mentally and emotionally* we are shielded from the distorting world views that such attacks can create in our souls.

c) *Spiritually* we are protected from the venomous poison that is intended to prevent the reality of our relationship with God as our Father.

Although the world is murderously hostile to sons of God, all sons of God are more than resourced and equipped to crush and destroy the head of the devil. Nevertheless, according to the prophecy, there shall be a bruising of the heel. This informs us that although the son cannot lose the war, in the battle there will be some bruising, some infliction of injury on the choice son. Since the injury prophesied is on the heel of the son, it does not alter the victorious outcome.

The bruising of the heel further suggests that the injury is sustained as the son is striking his victorious blow. Whether or not this is the case, some injury is prophesied to the son. We do well to understand that it is a real war with real physical casualties. Death, sickness and oppression are never acceptable; we however acknowledge that our battle is against an enemy without scruples. Our enemy will target the most vulnerable, the young, the old, and the disabled with dirty weapons of mass destruction, but the most he can do is bruise the heel.

In the final analysis the enemy is restricted by prophecy whereas we the believers are liberated by it: "*You shall know the truth and the truth shall make you free*" (John 8:32, NKJV). Prophecy declares the enemy shall come to an end with the crushing of his head. The Son however shall have no end; on the contrary, he shall continue His walk in victory.

> "*4 For everyone born of God overcomes the world. This is the victory that has overcome the world, even our faith. 5 Who is it that overcomes the world? Only the one who believes that Jesus is the Son of God. (1 John 5: 4,5, NIV)*

Your REFLECTIONS

List practical ways in which you can access these unlimited resources of the Kingdom.

Chapter 19: Perfect Army on Display

"⁹ After this I looked, and there before me was a great multitude that no one could count, from every nation, tribe, people and language, standing before the throne and before the Lamb. They were wearing white robes and were holding palm branches in their hands. ¹⁴ I answered, "Sir, you know." And he said, "These are they who have come out of the great tribulation; they have washed their robes and made them white in the blood of the Lamb." (Revelation 7: 9,14, NIV)

Our heavenly Father's elaborate and ingenious plan is to create an army that is 'Son'. This again captures His image of plurality in oneness. This army will comprise every nation, every ethnic group, every colour, every ability, every gender, every age: and yet this army of diversity will be one Son (in other words one body, which is the body of the Son). As according to His eternal plan, He who is Spirit, compelled by the fact that He is love, will have made His invisible self, visible in the physical realm. In the book of Revelation John is given a vision of this army of 'Son'.

There is no earthly reference for this sight, every example of troops on parade is pathetically inadequate. In this vision John saw wall to wall troops extending beyond the limits of sight. He saw the wonders of diversity and the perfect unity of oneness, moving in perfect symmetry. He saw innumerable sons of God. He saw the one and only

Son of God. John saw a victory parade of the army having crushed the head of its enemy. He saw the Son of God dressed in the perfect diversity of humanity, exactly representing the Father in the physical.

He saw more than the defeat of opposition: He saw the fulfilment of eternal purpose. The story does not end with our enemy being thrown into the lake of fire; there is rather a real beginning with the fulfilment of eternal purpose. John saw the Son of God on visible display in full glory dressed as perfected sons of men. He also saw the sons of men on spiritual display united together as sons of God in the one Son of God.

This concept of display is in synergy with the eternal plan of God and very much the only plan of God. For His plan from eternity, motivated by love, was to share His all-sufficient invisible self in visibility within the context of time and space. Using the English language as a play on phonetics "history" has always been "His story". It has never been merely centred on our fall and our redemption, which is only a means to an end. That sharing of Himself could only be realised in His Son.

The whole plan was fully choreographed in absolute detail before the beginning of time with only one inevitable result: that the Eternal invisible God would be on perfect display as the only visible Son.

The idea of God being shocked or surprised by the fall of man and having to come up with a second plan to rescue us, is false doctrine based on a God who is not all powerful or all present or all knowing. Such fallacy also assumes that He began the creation process without consistent objectives. As much as mankind has a significant role in God's eternal plan, if we are to truly grasp the wonders of the eternal plan of God, it is vital that we see the central character of the plan as the Eternal God Himself. Only by viewing history through this paradigm can we really begin to capture the complete story of God, understanding His love, grace, justice, and integrity.

It is critical to our understanding of the eternal purpose of God that we get the message: the purpose of God does not end with the destruction of the works of the devil, rather it is a new beginning. Satan is not at the centre of God's purpose. Sometimes we can be so focused on him within our church culture that we are inadvertently devil worshipping by giving him too much glory. Sin perverts our central focus. So often the negative becomes the central focus of our living until we begin to think that we cannot live without it. Some church meetings are so focused on the works and person of the devil that one might wonder if the meeting would have any purpose without it. A simple test is if we take the devil out of our meetings, how much content are we left with? I am not suggesting that there is no devil as the Bible is clear about our need to crush his very real head; what I am questioning is the proportion of our attention which he is securing due to his weapons of mass distraction.

"Be alert and of sober mind. Your enemy the devil prowls around like a roaring lion looking for someone to devour." (1 Peter 5:8, NIV)

We must also be mindful of not becoming so complacent that we are entertaining devils and demons rather than driving them out.

It is also critical that we understand that although we have a major role in God's eternal purpose, the eternal purpose does not end with our salvation, as we are not at the centre. The narrative that suggests that our salvation is the core goal of God's purpose would suggest that once all men that can be saved are saved then God's purpose is complete. Alternatively, even more incredulous if we follow this narrative, is the conclusion that before the fall God would have had no purpose since our need for salvation would have been unnecessary. The centre of God's eternal purpose is the eternal Son of God, there is no substitute.

"Jesus Christ is the same yesterday, today, and forever." (Hebrews 13:8, NLT)

The eternal purpose of God has perfect integrity. It has lost nothing through time and space, and it does not depend on time and space for its existence. All things are in existence because of His eternal purpose. God who always is and therefore is without causation is the cause of everything.

It is paramount that we understand Jesus the **Son of Man, Son of God** as the visible one sent as a spiritual ark to contain the many sons. The sons are fitted together in His body, as the church being a visible representation of an invisible God.

John describes his glimpse of this futuristic army in revelation, this overwhelming glorious sight as fulfilment of eternal purpose, the invisible God made visible in a numberless army of sons. This army is not a static army. It is a vast growing diverse creative living physical body, fulfilling the eternal purpose of the invisible Spirit God.

The army seen in revelation is not separate to the Son, this is the army of the Son, according to the Word of God.

"Truly I tell you, unless a grain of wheat falls to the ground and dies, it remains by itself. But if it dies, it produces much fruit." (John 12:24, CSB)

The grain of wheat did not choose to hold on to His life but rather like a lamb He sacrificed His life to create an army. This army is the result of the seed Jesus the Son of God being sown in the earth and dying to reconcile mankind to His Father.

The army spoken of in Revelation has come through a great battle with sin and death through an extremely hostile environment in which they have faced the full venomous rage of the enemy of their souls, Satan the devil. The army are dressed in a uniform made clean by the efficacious shed blood of Christ. Their very hearts have been stained with the pollution of sin. The blood of Jesus has reached into the depths of the infectious stain and cleansed from the inside out until the uniform is made whiter than snow. This army is plurality in one, it has many sons in the one Christ Son. It is the visible physical display of the invisible Spirit God who is also plurality in one, separate persons, Father Son and Holy Spirit and yet one God.

Your REFLECTIONS

Father in His plan has accounted for every breath of your life so you can forever be a part of His household. Meditate on this truth and make notes on what the Holy Spirit says to you.

Chapter 20: Walking in Sonship

> "*Then had the churches rest throughout all Judaea and Galilee and Samaria, and were edified; and walking in the fear of the Lord, and in the comfort of the Holy Ghost, were multiplied.*" (Acts 9:31, KJV)

As has been stated in previous chapters, the status of Son is not earned, it is the gift of God through the work of the Holy Spirit. Neither is it an option, it is the only position available in the Kingdom to the sons of men. God has no need for a back-up plan. We were originally created to be sons of God and although man lost his esteemed status through sin, God's intended purpose for us has not altered. There is no other role within the Kingdom of God for the sons of men. The reality is that sons of men can often identify with the returning son of Luke twenty-two. Our thoughts may sometimes flow a bit like this:

"*Why should God restore me to the esteemed status of Sonship when I have despised the gift of life and corrupted myself with sinful acts?*"

"*Why should God restore me to Sonship when I am so obviously weak? Let me occupy some lower status, I am not worthy of being a Sonship.*"

"*Then the great challenge is what happens when I fail, how can I accept the status of Sonship knowing that I will fail again? No, God does not understand; I cannot accept that kind of honour because I am comprised of flesh which is weak. I cannot accept this honour because I am a son of man. It is more expedient that I stay near the exit so I will not need to go too far to leave or be less of an embarrassment when I fail. If I accept the status of Sonship it is further to fall, 'so make me a hired servant.'"*

Our position as a son of God is not based on our thoughts and feelings, it is based on God's choice which is Jesus every time. God's choice for Sonship is Jesus; the Father declared, "*This is my beloved Son, with whom I am well-pleased.*" (Matthew 3:17, ESV).

Our position as a son of God is founded in Christ. God's declaration of us as a son is totally about His completed work in Christ. The returning son's error and often our mistake is that we assume that our restoration to Sonship is somehow connected to who we are or what we will do.

Both assumptions are often a fatal mistake; our restoration to Sonship is based on who Jesus is and what He has done. There is no Sonship outside of Christ and there is no other vacancy in the Kingdom of God for the sons of men except as sons of God. Yes, we receive this gift of God through exercising our faith, but our restoration to sons of God is totally due to the grace of God. God's choice of 'Son' is always Jesus; our salvation is only in Christ; Sonship is not an option for the believer.

> "[9] *This is how God showed his love among us: He sent his one and only Son into the world that we might live through him.* [10] *This is love: not that we loved God, but that he loved us and sent*

his Son as an atoning sacrifice for our sins. (1 John 4:9-10, NIV)

Our status as 'son of man' qualifies us to be recipients of the status 'Son of God' in the Kingdom. This is nothing to do with deserving the status, it is simply that God created sons of men to be sons of God. If you were another member of the animal kingdom or even a celestial being, you simply would not have the qualities necessary for 'son of God' status. This robe of flesh, which is forever pulling us towards the ground because of sin also marks our prerequisite identity as a son of man created to be a son of God.

The consequence of sin was not only the destiny of death but also an infection of death, which pulls us like a magnet towards itself. When we are saved by grace through faith, our destination is immediately changed from death to life, but our journey is still fraught with a continuous struggle against the infection of death in our flesh and in the world. It is this sense of corruption that makes us feel unworthy to wear the robe and the ring of 'son'.

Yet it is imperative that we understand that this same robe of flesh identifies us as a son of man designed to be a son of God. God is looking for sons made of spirit and wrapped in flesh; He is not looking for angels or creatures of the earth. He is looking to redeem corrupted sons of men. Our complete and utter wretchedness makes us ideal candidates for the demonstration of the glory and grace of God.

"For the Son of Man came to seek and save those who are lost." (Luke 19:10, NLT)

The first step in walking as a son of God is acknowledging that God has not made a mistake in choosing fallen men, that it was intentional from the beginning. We the sons of men were designed as His image bearers to be sons of God. Our robes of flesh identify us as perfect candidates to be recipients for the honoured status of 'son of God'.

The second step is understanding that our 'son of God' status is founded in Christ. Our Sonship is Christ Sonship. He is the container, and we are the contained. He is the head, and we are His body. He is the only begotten Son and fitted together in Him we are sons. It is folly to suggest we are Sons of God outside of a living relationship with Christ. Historical claims of being baptised or of past church involvement is as useful as any good works; there is no Sonship outside of Christ.

"But if we walk in the light, as he is in the light, we have fellowship with one another, and the blood of Jesus, his Son, purifies us from all sin." (1 John 1:7, NIV)

I have used the Acts 9:31 Scripture to re-emphasise in my concluding chapter that walking in Sonship is to walk in plurality. This scripture is speaking of the journey of the church. The idea of being a Son of God outside of the ecclesia, the called-out body of Christ, is unbiblical. The rationale that one's personal relationship with Jesus can make our relationship with other believers redundant, is a gross error in judgement.

A church in its organisational format can look different; we have a plethora of forms throughout the ages. Since the spirit of isolationism is a spirit of antiChrist and is against the purpose of God, it must be strongly resisted.

We have too many so-called believers who are sitting in isolation and refusing to receive or give fellowship to other believers with a notion that fellowship is optional. At the same time the spirit of isolationism can operate within local or mega churches as they insist on simply doing their own thing in exclusion to all other believers.

As has been stated in previous chapters, the status of 'son' is not earned, it is the gift of God through the work of the Holy Spirit. Neither is it an option, it is the only position available in the Kingdom to the sons of men. God has no need for a back-up plan.

Too many are being lost to sin, death, and hell because they are submitting to the demonic spirit of isolation rather than submitting themselves to God. The mantra of not needing the church is to be in opposition to God. John articulates this very clearly in his epistle when he poses the question: 'How can we love God who we cannot see and yet hate a brother who we can see?' We cannot purport to love God in our homes and then refuse to fellowship with the children of the same God, it is incompatible. The very notion that you can walk in God outside of His purpose is a curse. "*God is love.*" (1 John 4:8, NIV) Relationship is at the heart of love. Isolationism from other believers, whether with an individual or within a church organisation is the spirit of the antiChrist.

The third step in walking as a son is understanding our total reliance on the Holy Spirit. The walk of sons of God is designed for sons of men, yet it is completely beyond us because of the infection of death in the world and in our flesh. This not only seeks to pull our bodies into the grave, it also seeks to make us contagious to others through our works of corruption (otherwise known as the works of the flesh as described in Galatians 5:19-21).

Jesus set us the prime example by laying aside His glory, pouring Himself into vulnerable humanity, and living a life of total reliance on the Holy Spirit. As a son of man, through His moment by moment reliance on the Holy Spirit, He walked on earth perfectly as Son of God. Jesus was not pretending to be human. He was fully human, and as a full son of man, relying on the Holy Spirit, He walked righteously as the Son of God. In this He declared that the Holy Spirit is more than able to lead man with all his vulnerabilities victoriously through a fallen world. In this He declared that the only way to walk as a Son of God and as a son of man, was through complete reliance on the Holy Spirit. Keeping in step with the Holy Spirit is essential to our walk as sons of God.

In every way, walking as a Son of God is dependent on a living intimate relationship with the Holy Spirit. He has to be more than a theological thought, more than a Charismatic hug, and more than a Pentecostal power surge. There needs to be a person to person, spirit to Spirit, moment by moment reliance on Him.

For sons of men who have been born again as sons of God we need to acknowledge our complete destitution without Him and our total need of Him. David captured this in Psalm 51 when he said, *"don't take your Holy Spirit from me"* (Psalm 51:11, NLT). The walk of the sons of God is a walk in step with the Holy Spirit to the extent that you are walking in the Spirit of God.

Your REFLECTIONS

How do we embrace our humanity as positive, in Christ?

Chapter 21: Not in Conclusion

"Being confident of this very thing, that He who has begun a good work in you will complete it until the day of Jesus Christ." (Philippians 1:6, NKJV)

To reconcile humanity in its fundamental physicality and soulish context, with this awesome position of being a partaker of divinity as a Son of God, appears from the outset to be an impossible reach. It would be impossible to attain if it was merely a story of our attempt to achieve this lofty position in God. However, this is not about the plan of a limited being but of a supernatural God with only one ingenious plan that simply cannot fail because of who He is.

God's plan, from our severely flawed context, as we experience our own brokenness and the daily tragedies in our world, can appear as a fabricated dream, from one with little or much hope.

The key point to God's plan is that it began in God before time, and it uniquely depends on God through time and beyond time for its success.

"In the beginning God…" (Genesis 1:1, NIV)

The integrity of this plan cannot be corrupted, it was conceived in the inner sanctuary of the Eternal God and it depends totally on Him for completion. It cannot fail.

From the outset man was created to be a bridge between two realms. From his genesis man was physically formed of the earth but spiritually raised to live by the breath of God, designed to be His unique image bearer.

> *"Then the Lord God formed a man from the dust of the ground and breathed into his nostrils the breath of life, and the man became a living being."* (Genesis 2:7, NIV)

This is clearly recorded in the Scriptures: God's elaborate and ingenious plan is clearly seen throughout the records of time and regardless of the opposition, the plan continues to unfold. The seed of Sonship was there from the beginning and even before the beginning in Christ in God. Sons of men were always destined in the plan of God to be sons of God. This position was never dependent on the circumstance or frailty of man, but rather on the incorruptible integrity of God's eternal plan.

God's plan is ultimately a demonstration of His grace which is an illustration of His love. It is the revealing of His boundless generosity and kindness in a visible physical realm. As Sons of men, spiritual beings clothed in vulnerable flesh, we are specially designed and created for the central role as members of the body of Christ the Son of God on earth.

However, for every single son of man this depends on our individual faith response to the grace provision of God in Christ. Our emotional struggles and our inner conflict as humans are real, yet fundamentally irrelevant to who we are and who we are created to be. Our struggles and inner conflict neither lessen nor increase the reality of our identity in Christ. These emotions and conflicts are there to remind us of how dependent we are on the grace of God. In Christ we are **Son of Man, Son of God**.

This is not a conclusion, for the conclusion must be accomplished in you and with you.

If you have read this book in a group, keep the network or fellowship alive. If you have read it as an individual, develop a real support network. Please link into our network, for support and as a supporter. It is the most exciting thing to be walking in the intentional plan of God that will lead us from glory to glory. God bless you and thank you for taking the time to receive my gift through these pages.

Your REFLECTION

Write down 5 key areas you will work on going forward.

Congratulations for getting this far!

To receive the greatest value from what you have learned in **Son of Man, Son of God**, commit to returning to this manual, adding and reflecting on your personal and spiritual growth as you take action on what the Holy Spirit is teaching you.

Go ahead and invite your fellow leaders, team members and believers to get a copy of this life changing resource from Amazon via this

ISBN: 9798527830477

Course Facilitator's Guide

Suggested timing for remote programs: 60 minutes, on site programs: 75 minutes for more social interaction. (All this is dependent on group size).

Session Guide

- ➢ Opening Prayer
- ➢ General reflection on reading from individuals
- ➢ Discussion Questions
- ➢ Closing Prayer

Course Agenda

Session 1: WHO HAS HE CHOSEN?
Chapters 1 to 3

I. What challenges does your humanity present in your attempt to live for God?

II. Share something of where you are in your spiritual journey.

III. What are you doing with your inner drive for purpose?

Session 2: INTENTIONAL SPEECH

Chapters 4 to 5

   I. What does the relationship Father/Son mean to you?

   II. Explain why God must be intentional.

   III. Can you identify some examples of how God has been intentional in your life?

Session 3: PERFECT MEDIATOR

Chapters 6 to 9

   I. What did you experience or hear from the sacred moment in the prayer of Jesus in John 17?

   II. What makes Jesus the perfect mediator?

   III. What does being a son in relationship with God as Father in Christ mean to you?

Session 4: THE BIRTH OF SONS

Chapters 10 to 13

   I. We have been given access to the executive. What do you understand by this? How does this apply to your life?

   II. Partakers of oneness - how does this translate in terms of your practical experiences of church?

   III. What do you understand by 'sonship' being our only available position in the Kingdom?

Session 5: GREATER WORKS THAN THESE

Chapters 14 to 16

I. What difference does it make to you to be in the Age of the Son?

II. How have you encountered the person of the Holy Spirit?

III. How do you walk with authority in your everyday life?

Session 6: THY KINGDOM COME

Chapters 17 to 19

I. How would you define the Kingdom of God?

II. What do we mean by a hostile environment, and why is it particularly directed against the Son?

III. What has been your experience of this hostile environment? How have you overcome? What resources have you used in your struggles?

IV. How does it change your perspective when you think about God's eternal plan and you being part of the army?

V. 'Purpose is fulfilled in the coming of the kingdom'; what does that mean?

Session 7: WORD BECOMING FLESH

Chapters 20 to 21

I. How has this journey been for you?

II. Recount how you have heard the voice of the Father resonate in your spirit throughout these sessions.

III. How will you carry forward this conversation with God as Father?

IV. What practical things will you do differently? What will you change?

V. What has changed in your perspective?

About the Author

Maurice Kennedy is married to Sharon and together they have raised four adult children. He is a graduate in Theology from NTCG Bible college. The author also holds a BA Hons in Professional Studies and Education from Sussex University, and a Postgraduate degree as an Adult Educator and Trainer from Greenwich University.

The author loves to read novels and is particularly drawn to the creativity of a multi-layered story. He believes the life of Christ is the greatest multi-layered story ever. Maurice is excited to be the author of this book about Jesus. With a passion for enabling and developing people to achieve their full potential, the author has served in various churches, discipling, preaching, pastoring, and teaching, for over thirty years. He is currently pastoring in Petra Church UK.

Maurice has also served extensively in the community, developing and delivering parenting projects, learning disability training, alongside health and social care professional courses. He is honoured to be on this journey with you, even as you have chosen to read this book.

It is from this eclectic experience that Maurice Kennedy feels honoured to be chosen to share on such a vital subject regarding our purpose and position in God, **Son of Man, Son of God**.

Connect with the author at E: kennedywrites88@aol.com

FB: https://www.facebook.com/maurice.kennedy.148/

Printed in Great Britain
by Amazon